99-113

131-162

A SHORTER *SUMMA*

PETER KREEFT

A Shorter *Summa*

The Most Essential
Philosophical Passages
of St. Thomas Aquinas'

Summa Theologica

*Edited and Explained
for Beginners*

IGNATIUS PRESS   SAN FRANCISCO

Passages from the *Summa Theologica*
are taken from the translation done in 1920 by
The Fathers of the English Dominican Province.
Used with permission.

Cover painting by Gozzoli
Saint Thomas Aquinas
Photo by CNF/KNA

Cover design by Roxanne Mei Lum

ISBN 0-89870-438-3
Library of Congress catalogue number 92-75065
Printed in the United States of America

To Norris W. Clark, S.J.

More than a great Thomist;
A little Thomas

CONTENTS

I. METHODOLOGY:
THEOLOGY AS A SCIENCE

II. PROOFS FOR THE EXISTENCE OF GOD

III. THE NATURE OF GOD

IV. COSMOLOGY:
CREATION AND PROVIDENCE

V. ANTHROPOLOGY: BODY AND SOUL

Of Man Who Is Composed of a Spiritual and a Corporeal Substance: and in the First Place, concerning What

CONTENTS

PREFACE

This is a shortened version of *Summa of the Summa*, which in turn was a shortened version of the *Summa Theologiae* (or *Summa Theologica*). The reason for the double shortening is pretty obvious: the original runs some 3000 pages! (The *Summa of the Summa* was just over 500.)

The *Summa* is certainly the greatest, most ambitious, most rational book of theology ever written. In it, there is also much philosophy, which is selected, excerpted, arranged, introduced, and explained by footnotes here.

St. Thomas expresses the medieval mind par excellence. Not to know him at all is to be ignorant of the most important intellectual development between 384 B.C. (the death of Aristotle) and 1637 A.D. (the publication of Descartes' *Discourse on Method*)—over 2000 years.

This little book is designed for beginners, either for classroom use or individually. It contains the most famous and influential samples of St. Thomas' philosophy with copious aids to understanding them, as explained in the longer Introduction that follows.

INTRODUCTION

> I couldn't make any judgment on the *Summa*, except to say
> this: I read it every night before I go to bed. If my mother
> were to come in during the process and say, "Turn off that
> light. It's late," I with lifted finger and broad bland beatific
> expression, would reply, "On the contrary, I answer that the
> light, being eternal and limitless, cannot be turned off. Shut
> your eyes," or some such thing. In any case I feel I can per-
> sonally guarantee that St. Thomas loved God because for the
> life of me I cannot help loving St. Thomas.
>
> — Flannery O'Connor, *The Habit of Being*

I. ON ST. THOMAS

St. Thomas Aquinas is certainly one of the greatest philosophers who ever lived (to my mind he is *the* greatest), for at
least eight reasons: truth, common sense, practicality, clarity, profundity, orthodoxy, medievalism, and modernity.

First, and most simply, he told the truth—that simple
and unfashionable purpose of philosophy that is so often
fudged ("nuanced") or forgotten today. The following quo-
tation should be chiseled on the doorposts of every philosophy department in the world: "The study of philosophy
is not the study of what men have opined, but of what is the
truth."

2. Descartes says that the one thing he learned about philosophy in the university that stuck with him was that one
could not imagine any doctrine so bizarre or unbelievable
that it has not been seriously taught by some philosopher
or other. What was true already in 1637 is triply true today. St. Thomas, however, is the master of common sense.
He has an uncanny knack of sniffing out the obviously right

position amid a hundred wrong ones. This holds true especially in ethics, the real test of a philosopher. Some great philosophers, like Descartes, Hegel, and Heidegger, have no philosophical ethics at all. Others, like Hobbes and Hume and Kant and Nietzsche, have ethics that are simply unlivable. St. Thomas is as practical and plain and reasonable in ethics as Aristotle, or Confucius, or your uncle.

3. St. Thomas was a master of metaphysics and technical terminology; yet he was also such a practical man that as he lay dying he was talking about three things: a commentary on *The Song of Songs*, a treatise on aqueducts, and a dish of herring. Ordinary people, Popes, and kings wrote to him for advice and always got back sound wisdom. I know of no one since St. Paul who is so full of both theoretical *and* practical wisdom.

4. Those who love truth passionately usually also love simplicity and clarity of style so that as many people as possible can benefit from this precious thing, Truth. Fr. Norris Clarke, S.J. of Fordham University, the most Aquinas-like mind I know of all men living, says there are three kinds of philosophers: those who at first seem clear, but upon further readings become more and more obscure; those who at first may seem obscure but become clearer and clearer upon each reading (St. Thomas is the prime example of this kind), and those who seem obscure at first and remain obscure.

St. Thomas aimed only for light, not heat. There is almost never anything personal in the *Summa*, no rhetoric, no appeal to the irrational; nothing but lucidity.

5. And depth—no philosopher since St. Thomas has ever so successfully combined the two fundamental ideals of philosophical writing: clarity and profundity. Continental European philosophy in this century has sought and sometimes found depth, by focusing on the truly fundamental issues, but at the expense of clarity. English philosophy has sought and often found clarity, but at the expense of depth, concentrating on second-order linguistic questions rather

than on those the average person wonders at: God, man, life, death, good, and evil.

6. A sixth reason for St. Thomas' greatness is decisive only for Catholics, but it should at least be decisive for *all* Catholics: according to the Church's own teaching authority (and to be a Catholic *means* to believe in such a thing), St. Thomas is the primary theological Doctor (Teacher) of the Church. During its proceedings, the Council of Trent placed the *Summa* on the high altar in second place only to the Bible. Pope Leo XIII in *Aeterni Patris* (1879) told all Catholic teachers to "restore the golden wisdom of St. Thomas . . . and let them clearly point out its solidity and excellence above all other teaching".

Even non-Catholics must go to St. Thomas to understand Catholic theology and philosophy. You can never understand a philosophy from its critics or dissenters. In four colleges and universities, I have never had a good course on any philosopher (including many philosophers I disagree with) from a critic, and never a worthless one from a disciple.

7. St. Thomas was crucial for the medieval era. He fulfilled more than anyone else the essential medieval program of a marriage of faith and reason, revelation and philosophy, the Biblical and the classical inheritances. In so doing, he held together for another century the medieval civilization's intellectual soul, which in his century was threatening to break up like a ship battered by huge waves of division, caused mainly by the rediscovery of the works of Aristotle and the polarization of reactions into the fearful heresy-hunting of traditionalists, and the fashionable compromising of modernists. Aquinas stands as a shining example of an alternative to both the fundamentalists and the liberals of his day and of any day.

You may not agree that St. Thomas is history's greatest philosopher, but he was certainly the greatest philosopher for the two thousand years between Aristotle and Descartes. He represents the medieval mind par excellence, and the Middle

Ages are the parent and source of all the divergent streams in the modern world, like a mother whose many children went their own various ways.

Not only does St. Thomas represent a unity of ingredients that were later to separate, but also a unity of ingredients that existed separately before him. In reading St. Thomas you also meet Thales, Parmenides, Heraclitus, Socrates, Plato, Aristotle, Plotinus, Proclus, Justin, Clement, Augustine, Boëthius, Dionysius, Anselm, Abelard, Albert, Maimonides, and Avicenna. For one brief, Camelot-like moment it seemed that a synthesis was possible. Our fractured world has been praying "Forgive us our syntheses" ever since.

8. Finally, St. Thomas is important for us today precisely because of our lack. Timeless truth is always timely, of course, but some aspects of truth are especially needed at some times, and it seems that our times badly need seven Thomistic syntheses: (1) of faith and reason, (2) of the Biblical and the classical, the Judeo-Christian and the Greco-Roman heritages, (3) of the ideals of clarity and profundity, (4) of common sense and technical sophistication, (5) of theory and practice, (6) of an understanding, intuitive vision and a demanding, accurate logic, and (7) of the one and the many, a cosmic unity or "big picture" and carefully sorted out distinctions. I think it a safe judgment that no one in the entire history of human thought has ever succeeded better than St. Thomas in making not just one but all seven of these marriages which are essential to mental health and happiness.

For some reason, many people seem so threatened by St. Thomas that they instantly label any admiration for, use of, or learning from him as slavish, unoriginal, and authoritarian—something that they do with no other thinker. Of course St. Thomas cannot be the be-all and end-all of our thought. He cannot be an end, but he can be a beginning, like Socrates. Of course we must go beyond him and not slavishly confine our thought to his. But there is no better bottom story to our edifice of thought.

II. ON THE *SUMMA THEOLOGICA*

Many theologians and philosophers in St. Thomas' time wrote Summas. A Summa is simply a summary. It is more like an encyclopedia than a textbook, and it is meant to be used more as a reference library than as a book. There is extreme economy in the use of words. There are no digressions and few illustrations. Everything is "bottom line". Such a style should appeal to us busy moderns.

The medievals had a passion for order, because they believed that *God* had a passion for order when He designed the universe. So a Summa is ordered and outlined with loving care. Yet, though very systematic, a Summa is not *a system* in the modern sense, a closed and deductive system like that of Descartes, Spinoza, Leibniz, or Hegel. It uses induction as well as deduction, and its data come from ordinary experience and divine revelation as well as philosophical axioms ("first principles").

A Summa is really a summarized debate. To the medieval mind, debate was a fine art, a serious science, and a fascinating entertainment, much more than it is to the modern mind, because the medievals believed, like Socrates, that dialectic could uncover truth. Thus a "scholastic disputation" was not a personal contest in cleverness, nor was it "sharing opinions"; it was a shared journey of discovery. The "objections" from the other side are to be taken seriously in a Summa. They are not straw men to be knocked down easily, but live options to be considered and learned from. St. Thomas almost always finds some important truth hidden in each objection, which he carefully distinguishes from its error. For he believed not only that there was all truth Somewhere but also that there was some truth everywhere.

The structural outline of the *Summa Theologica* is a mirror of the structural outline of reality. It begins in God, Who is "in the beginning". It then proceeds to the act of creation and a consideration of creatures, centering on man, who alone is created in the image of God. Then it moves to man's return to God through his life of moral and religious choice, and culminates in the way or means to that end: Christ and His Church. Thus the overall scheme of the *Summa*, like that of the universe, is an *exitus-redditus*, an exit from and a return to God, Who is both Alpha and Omega. God is the ontological heart that pumps the blood of being through the arteries of creation into the body of the universe, which wears a human face, and receives it back through the veins of man's life of love and will. The structure of the *Summa*, and of the universe, is dynamic. It is not like information in a library, but like blood in a body.

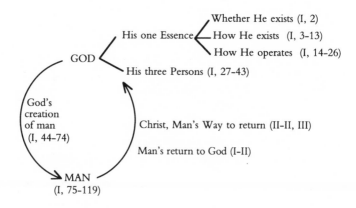

It is essential to keep this "big picture" in mind when reading the *Summa* because there are so many details that it is tempting to focus on them and lose the sense of their place and order. St. Thomas never does that. His style is atomistic and "choppy" but his vision is continuous and all-encompassing.

Why is the style so choppy? St. Thomas chops his prose into bite-sized segments for the same reason Mommy cuts Baby's meat into bite-sized chunks. The *Summa* would lose much of its clarity and digestibility if it were homogenized into continuous, running prose, like watery stew. (A current British version has done just that.)

The best preparation for reading the *Summa* is a review of basic, common sense logic, i.e., Aristotelian logic, especially the "Three Acts of the Mind", as the medievals labeled them: understanding, judging, and reasoning, with their respective logical expressions: terms, propositions, and arguments. The reader will be constantly confused if he does not first have in his mind a very clear idea of the differences between terms (which are either clear or unclear), propositions (which are either true or false), and arguments (which are either logically valid or invalid). He should also have a clear idea of the structure of a syllogism, the basic form of deductive argument, which connects the subject and predicate terms of its conclusion through the middle term in its two premises, the first of which (the major premise) states a general principle and the second (the minor premise) brings a particular case under that principle. The conclusion then demonstrates the result of applying the general principle to the particular case.

A knowledge of the basic ideas and technical terms of Aristotle's philosophy, which St. Thomas used as his philosophical language, is also essential. For beginners I recommend Mortimer Adler's amazingly clear *Aristotle for Everybody*, and for intermediate students W. D. Ross' one-volume *Aristotle*.

The *Summa Theologica* is divided into four overall Parts (I, I–II, II–II, and III). Each Part is divided into Treatises (e.g., On the Creation, On Man, On Law). Each Treatise is divided into numbered "Questions", or general issues within the topic of the treatise (e.g., "Of the Simplicity of God", "Of the Angels in Comparison with Bodies", "Of the Effects of Love"). Finally, each "Question" is divided into numbered "Articles". The "Article" is the basic thought-unit of the *Summa*. What we mean in modern English by an "article"—an essay—is what St. Thomas means by a

"Question", and what we mean by a "question"—a specific, single interrogative sentence—is what he means by an "Article", e.g., "Whether God Exists, "Whether the Inequality of Things Is from God?", "Whether Sorrow Is the Same as Pain?"

Each Article begins by formulating in its title a single question in such a way that only two answers are possible: yes or no. St. Thomas does this, not because he thinks philosophy or theology is as simple as a true-false exam, but because he wants to make an issue finite and decidable, just as debaters do in formulating their "resolution". There are an indefinite number of possible answers to a question like "What is God?" If he had formulated his questions that way, the *Summa* might be three million pages long instead of three thousand. Instead, he asks, for example, "Whether God Is a Body?" It is possible to decide and demonstrate that one of the two possible answers (yes) is false and therefore that the other (no) is true.

Each "Article" has five structural parts. First, the question is formulated in a yes or no format, as explained above, beginning with the word "Whether" (*Utrum*).

Second, St. Thomas lists a number of Objections (usually three) to the answer he will give. The Objections are apparent proofs of this opposite answer, the other side to the debate. These objections begin with the formula: "It seems that . . ." (*Oportet*). These Objections must be *arguments*, not just *opinions*, for one of the basic principles of any intelligent debate (woefully neglected in all modern media) is that each debater *must* give relevant *reasons* for every controvertible opinion he expresses. The Objections are to be taken seriously, as *apparent* truth. One who is seeking the strongest possible arguments against any idea of St. Thomas will rarely find any stronger ones, any more strongly argued, than those in St. Thomas himself. He is extremely fair to all his opponents. I think he descends to name-calling only once in the entire *Summa*, when he speaks of the "really stupid" idea of David of Dinant that God is indistinguishable from prime matter, or pure potentiality—an idea not far from that of Hegel and modern "process theologians"! (See S.T. I, 3, 8).

Third, St. Thomas indicates his own position with the formula "On the contrary . . ." (*Sed contra*). The brief argument that follows the statement of his position here is usually an argument from authority, i.e., from Scripture, the Fathers of the Church, or recognized wise men. The medievals well knew their own maxim that "the argument from authority is the weakest of all arguments" (see S.T. I, 1, 8, obj. 2). But they also believed in doing their homework and in learning from their ancestors—two habits we would do well to cultivate today.

The fourth part, "I answer that" (*Respondeo dicens*), is the body of the Article. In it, St. Thomas proves his own position, often adding necessary background explanations and making needed distinctions along the way. The easiest (but not the most exciting) way to read a *Summa* Article is to read this part first.

Fifth and finally, each Objection must be addressed and answered—not merely by repeating an argument to prove the opposite conclusion, for that has already been done in the body of the Article, but by explaining where and how the Objection went wrong, i.e., by distinguishing the truth from the falsity in the Objection.

No one of these five steps can be omitted if we want to have good grounds for settling a controverted question. If our question is vaguely or confusedly formulated, our answer will be, too. If we do not consider opposing views, we spar without a partner and paw the air. If we do not do our homework, we only skim the shallows of our selves. If we do not prove our thesis, we are dogmatic, not critical. And if we do not understand and refute our opponents, we are left with nagging uncertainty that we have missed something and not really ended the contest.

Like Socratic dialogue for Plato, this medieval method of philosophizing was very fruitful in its own day—and then subsequently neglected, especially in our day. That is one of the unsolved mysteries of Western thought. Surely both the Socratic and the Thomistic methodological trees can still bear much good fruit. Perhaps what stands in the way is our craze for originality and our proud refusal to be anyone's apprentice. I for one would be very happy to be Aquinas' apprentice, or Socrates'.

III. ON THIS BOOK

A. Its Need. This book differs from all other books on St. Thomas because it has all four of the following characteristics: it is (1) an anthology of St. Thomas' own words, not a secondary source textbook. (2) It is one that uses the old, *literal* Dominican translation, originally published in America by Benziger Brothers, rather than the hubristic paraphrases of some subsequent non-literal translators who succumb to the itch to insert their own interpretative mind and style between the author and the reader. I hope the modern reader is more charmed than annoyed at the old-fashioned formal literalness of the translation and at the old-fashioned punctuation. (3) It is one that confines itself to the *Summa* alone (for a single book is a unit like a work of art); and, most importantly, (4) it is one that is replete with explanatory footnotes (more on this feature below).

There are some excellent books *about* St. Thomas by the likes of Chesterton, Gilson, Maritain, Pieper, and McInerney, but nothing can substitute for the primary source itself. Secondary source books without St. Thomas always miss something crucial; St. Thomas without them does not.

It is even easier to understand St. Thomas than to understand some books about St. Thomas. Thomas is clearer than Thomists. I have read some fifty or sixty books about St. Thomas, but I never really understood or appreciated him until I read a lot of St. Thomas himself. I find it easier to understand Thomists through Thomas than to understand Thomas through Thomists. The primary source illuminates the secondary sources more than the secondary sources illuminate the primary source.

Part of the reason for this is that St. Thomas' *habits* of mental clarity rub off best from long and direct contact with his writings. I noticed a remarkable improvement in my mental sharpness and order after doing long and slow readings of St. Thomas. The Master's habits rub off on his apprentices, if they have the good sense to stay close to him.

More doctoral dissertations have been written on St. Thomas than on any other philosopher or theologian who ever lived. Thomism was taught extensively in all Catholic and some non-Catholic schools until the Silly Sixties, when everything older than thirty fell prey to the jaws of Woodstockism. Over 99 percent of the books written on St. Thomas in this century have gone out of print. But we are now seeing a modest but steady revival of interest in and books about this philosopher—a development to which this book is very happy to contribute.

B. Its Format. Good anthologies, unlike good surgery, have to cut away much healthy tissue. To keep this volume manageably small, I had to be severely selective with the *Summa*'s three thousand pages. The principle for choosing which passage to include was its likely use, both in class by students and teachers, and by the independent reader with general intelligence but without the professional background of the philosopher or the theologian. To this end, I included only passages that are both (1) intrinsically important and (2) nontechnical enough to be intelligible to modern readers. If a passage was important yet technical, I included it but also included explanatory footnotes.

Many, but not all, of the *Objections* St. Thomas lists and replies to are omitted because they are no longer live options or they no longer worry philosophers today. The Objections were real, actually debated questions in St. Thomas' day, and some should be the same for us. Not all are omitted because not all are dead issues by any means and also because it is essential to see the form of the *Summa* as a real, living dialogue, a structured and summarized debate, rather than a monologue or one-sided intellectual armory.

I also omitted all topics suitable for theology but not philosophy classes, i.e., the revealed as distinct from the rational, philosophical theology. This meant omitting all of Part III. The *Summa*, of course, is a work of theology rather than of philosophy, but it is appropriate to study it in a philosophy class because (1) it covers many other topics than God (e.g., man, knowledge, and morality), and because (2) even when it is about God, it uses strictly rational, philosophical arguments based on logical principles and empirical data as well as often using appeals to the data of divine revelation accepted by faith; and St. Thomas is always quite clear about the distinction between these two methods of knowing.

The most important feature of the format is the *footnotes*. These are an attempt to bridge the gap between a secondary source textbook which is a substitute for the primary text, on the one hand, and a mere, unadorned anthology on the other hand. They are the printed equivalent of the traditional classroom technique so often used on classics, *explicatio texti*.

I know no reason why this simple and obvious device of many footnotes has not been used much more, except for an irrational prejudice against the atomistic, choppy prose style that a plethora of footnotes produces. But that is the style of the *Summa* in the first place. Remember, Mommy cuts up your meat into bite-sized chunks. Beginners would do well to copy A.A.'s slogan "One Day at a Time" and study the *Summa* One Point at a Time.

Why so *many* footnotes instead of longer, more general

introductory essays for each section? (1) Because with St. Thomas general ideas are not adequate, though they are necessary; we need to understand him in specific detail; (2) because we need help understanding specific passages, which general introductions cannot supply; and (3) because this technique trains our minds, which all too often are accustomed to be satisfied with vague generalities, especially in philosophy and theology. St. Thomas thought of philosophy and theology as *sciences*. As a philosophy teacher I repeatedly discover that science majors find St. Thomas easier (at least at first) than humanities majors (especially sociology, psychology, and communications majors).

There are two different kinds of footnotes. Some explain the meaning of a difficult or technical idea. Others highlight the *importance* of an idea.

If a passage has no footnotes, that does not mean it is not important. Perhaps its meaning and importance are both very considerable, but clear.

There are more footnotes toward the beginning, for two reasons: (1) to prime the pump, to start the reader securely; and (2) because the first two Questions of the *Summa* are crucially important, both in themselves and as the foundation for the rest of the *Summa*; they are justly famous, and they need extra "unpacking".

Using the footnotes should not be felt as an onerous responsibility, but as a helpful aid, to be used only as needed and wanted. If they become a distraction from St. Thomas' text, ignore them.

If you as a reader get to the point in your reading of this book where the many footnotes begin to seem alien and intrusive, that is either a very good sign or a bad one. To find out which it is, ask yourself: "Alien and intrusive" *to what*? To the mind of the medieval author, or to the preconceptions of the modern reader? To St. Thomas or to yourself?

The whole purpose of these footnotes, as of all secondary source literature, is to serve as a crutch: to help you to walk yourself into the mind of the primary source, just as the purpose of a crutch is to become superfluous.

In any case, you should read the whole article in St. Thomas first, without reading the footnotes. Then read it a second time, more carefully and analytically, using the footnotes. A third reading can also dispense with the footnotes because they are now in the mind that is doing the reading.

Technical terms have been defined in the Glossary. The Glossary is very important because nearly all students' difficulties with St. Thomas are with the *terminology*, rather than with the *vision* (or content) or with the logical *form* (or style) of argument. The Glossary is put first because if it were put last, the reader would be tempted to ignore it except in emergencies. Placed first, it stands as a gate or door: a plain, dull door to a great, golden mansion.

GLOSSARY

abstract (opposite: *concrete*): not necessarily "spiritual" as vs. "material", but some property, quality, or essence considered apart from the subject, thing, or substance that possesses it (e.g., justice, redness).

abstraction: the mental act of apprehending some form, quality, or essence without the rest of the object; considering a form without considering the whole, concrete material object or the image (*phantasm*) of it; e.g., abstracting the essential treeness, or the accidental bigness, of a tree from everything else in the concrete individual tree or what we see of it.

accident (opposite: *substance*): that mode of being which can exist only in another being, as a modification or attribute of a substance (thing); e.g. the redness of a rose.

accidental: non-essential; non-substantial.

actual (opposite: *potential*): fully real, complete, perfect. (1) "*first act*": existence, being, actuality; (2) "*second act*": operation, doing, activity.

agent: efficient cause.

agent intellect: the intellect in the act of abstracting form from matter; the intellect that informs and determines the potential, passive, or possible (receptive) intellect with this form.

analogical: the relationship between two things or terms which are partly the same and partly different, neither *univocal* (wholly the same) nor *equivocal* (wholly different); the relationship of similarity but not identity between the meaning of a term when predicated of one subject (e.g., "milk is good") and the meaning of that term when predicated of another subject (e.g., "God is good").

appetite: in the widest sense, any inclination or tendency to some good or suitable object, or away from some bad or unsuitable object; more narrowly, in living things, the tendency to growth and health; still more narrowly, in animals, the senses' desire for their natural object (see *concupiscible appetite* and *irascible appetite*); most narrowly, in man, the will's desire for its proper good, *happiness.*

argument: a proof that a certain proposition (the conclusion) is true by showing (demonstrating) that it follows logically and necessarily from other propositions (premises) being true.

being: (1) that which is, whether actual or potential and whether in the mind (a "being of reason") or in objective reality (a "being in nature"); (1A) *ens:* entity, thing, substance, that which is; (1B) *esse:* the act of existing; (1C) *essentia:* essence, *what* a thing is; (2) the affirmative predicate "is" stating that the subject is, or is something (the predicate).

body: not just a human body, or an animal body, but any material thing that occupies space.

causality: influence of one being on another; responsibility of one being for some feature in another (the effect), such as its existence, its essence, its matter, its accidents, or its changes. See *final cause, formal cause, efficient cause, material cause.* In modern parlance "cause" usually means only "efficient cause", i.e., that which produces existence or change in another.

change: actualization of a potency.

charity: the will to do good to another for his own sake.

common (opposite: *proper*): present in two or more individuals or species.

concrete (opposite: *abstract*): not necessarily material or sensible, but individual and actual.

contemplative: see *speculative.*

concupiscence: sense appetite seeking pleasure.

corporeal: pertaining to the body as distinct from the soul.

cosmos: the universe as ordered.

creation: the act of bringing a being into existence from non-existence; production of being from no pre-existing material.

deduction: argument from a more universal premise to a more particular conclusion, from a general principle to an instance or application of it.

demonstration: logically valid argument from premises that are true and evident, thus proving the conclusion with certainty.

determine: to cause some definite perfection; to specify, to make particular.

efficient cause: agent which by its acting produces existence or change in another.

emanation: flowing forth from a source.

end: good, goal, purpose, aim, objective.

epistemology: the science of knowing.

equivocal term: a term used with two wholly different meanings.

essence: in the broad sense, *what* a thing is, all its "intelligible notes" (characteristics) (as contrasted with its *existence*); in the narrow sense, as vs. *accidents*, the definition, or genus plus specific difference of a thing, that without which it cannot be conceived.

eternity: mode of existence without beginning, end, or succession; "the whole and perfect simultaneous possession of limitless life" (Boëthius).

existence: the actuality of an essence, that act by which something *is.*

faculty: inherent power or ability.

final cause: end or purpose of a thing.

finite: limited.

form: the essential nature of a thing, that which specifies it to be this rather than that.

formal cause: form as determining matter.

genus: the aspect of a thing's essence which is common to it and other members of its species; a broader class to which a thing essentially belongs (e.g., "animal" for man, "plane figure" for triangle).

grace: that which comes from God's free will, as distinct from natural necessity.

habit: disposition toward certain operations; inclination to an end. A "habit" is not a "rut", but is freely made, in man, by repeated acts.

happiness: satisfaction of desire in really possessing its true and proper good. (Note that there is both a subjective and an objective element in happiness; thus neither a stone nor an evil man can be happy.)

idea: concept.

image: representation or likeness.

imagination: internal sense which produces images of sensible, material things even when they are absent.

incorporeal: immaterial, without body.

incorruptible: incapable of decay or destruction.

individual: that which cannot be divided without losing its identity.

induction: reasoning from individual cases to general principles, from more particular premises to more universal conclusions.

infallible: incapable of error, thus certain.

inference: reasoning from some truths (premises) to others (conclusions).

infinite: unlimited.

infused: received from without.

innate: inborn, given by nature.

irascible appetite: sense desire to fight a danger.

judgment: act of the mind comparing two concepts (subject and predicate) in an affirmative or negative proposition.

life: the power of a substance to move itself.

locomotion: motion in space.

matter: the principle in a thing's being by which it is able to be determined by form; potency as vs. actuality. In modern parlance, the word refers to actual, visible, formed things (e.g., chemicals, molecules); but in Thomistic and Aristotelian parlance "matter" is not of itself observable or even of itself actual. It is not a thing but a metaphysical principle or aspect of things, which together with form explains change, as the actualization (in-form-ing) of potency (matter).

material cause: that (potency) from which a thing is produced —e.g., the clay of a pot.

mean: something in the middle between two extremes.

metaphysics: that division of philosophy which studies being as such, and the universal truths, laws, or principles of all beings; "the science of being qua being".

motion: broadly, any change; more narrowly, change of place, or locomotion.

natural: (1) as vs. *artificial*: found in nature, what a being has from birth, what happens by itself without outside interference (art or violence); (2) as vs. *supernatural*: what is or happens without direct, divine intervention; (3) as vs. *rational*: without intelligence (e.g., "natural bodies"); (4) as vs. *arbitrary* or *conventional*: what flows from a thing's essence; necessary.

nature: (1) the origin of growth and activity in a thing; (2) the totality of objects in the universe apart from human or divine modifications of them.

necessary: what cannot be otherwise.

nominal (as vs. *real*): pertaining to a name only. "Nominalism" is the theory that universal terms like "justice" or "man" are only names, not real essences; it is perhaps the most pervasive and destructive error in modern philosophy.

participation: sharing in, possessing some perfection of.

passion: in general, receptivity, being acted on by another; in particular, intense movement of the sensitive appetite.

passive: in potency to be determined by another agent.

patient: any being that is changed by an agent.

perfection: most generally, any definite actuality in a being; more particularly, any definite *good* suitable to a being; most particularly, complete good attained by a being.

phantasm: sense image.

philosophy: literally, the love of wisdom; the science that seeks to understand all things by knowing their causes by natural reason.

possible: that which can be.

potency, or *potentiality:* the principle of change; capacity or ability to be actualized in some way.

predicate: (noun): term that says something about the subject; (verb): to state something about a subject.

principle: source; that from which something proceeds.

proper: distinctive, special, specific (as vs. *common*).

property: "proper accident", an attribute that is not the very essence of the subject but results from its essence (e.g., speech in man or greenness in chlorophyll).

proposition: declarative sentence, affirmative or negative.

providence: intelligent plan by which things are ordered to an end.

prudence: practical wisdom, knowing how to choose good means to good ends, what to do and how to do it. It has none of the prudish, prune-like, over-careful connotations of the word in modern parlance.

quiddity: whatness, essence.

reason: (1) most generally, that which distinguishes man from brute animals: intelligence; (2) more specifically, the power of reasoning (all three "acts of the mind": conceiving, judging, and arguing); (3) most specifically, the power to argue or prove (the "third act of the mind").

reduction: the mental act of bringing something complex back to a more fundamental or elementary form or principle, or seeing it within a general principle or class.

science: intellectual knowledge by means of causes or general principles. In one way, "scientific" meant something narrower and tougher in pre-modern times: certain knowledge of real causes. In another way, it meant something broader and looser than the modern scientific method, for it did not always require experimentation or mathematical measurement.

sensation: act of one of the five senses.

simple: not composed of parts.

sin: any human act (deed, word, or deliberate desire) in disobedience to divine law.

soul: generally, the first intrinsic (inner, natural) principle of life in a living body; specifically, the human soul is the first principle of human, rational life, i.e., of knowing and willing.

species: (1) in logic, the class to which a thing essentially belongs, expressing both the genus and the specific difference (e.g., "man is a rational animal"); (2) in epistemology, a likeness or representation of an object, the form of an object known.

specify: to determine to a definite form or class.

speculative (opposite of *practical*): contemplative; knowledge for the sake of knowledge, seeking the truth for its own sake rather than for action (doing something with it) or production (making something by it). "Speculative" does not necessarily mean "uncertain" or "hypothetical".

subject: (1) in logic, the term in a proposition about which something is said in the predicate; (2) in metaphysics, a substance in relation to attributes; (3) in epistemology, a knower as distinct from an object known.

substance: a being that exists in itself rather than in another (as vs. *accident*).

supernatural: beyond the power of nature, caused by God alone without secondary (natural) causes.

syllogism: (1) logical argument; (2) especially a deductive argument; (3) especially a certain deductive argument, with three terms, two premises, and one conclusion.

term: (1) in metaphysics, the first or last point of a series; (2) in logic, the subject or predicate of a proposition, expressing a concept.

transcendent: greater than, superior to.

transcendental: universally common to all things. The five transcendental properties of all being are: something, one, true, good, beautiful.

truth: conformity of the mind to real things.

universal: general, common to many.

univocal: having the same meaning when predicated of different things.

virtual: having an active, positive potency to some perfection; more than merely passively potential, but less than actual.

virtue: good habit.

will: rational appetite; power of the soul to desire or choose a good known by the intellect.

I. METHODOLOGY:
THEOLOGY AS A SCIENCE

Prologue

Because the Master[1] of Catholic Truth ought not only to teach the proficient, but also to instruct beginners (according to the Apostle: As Unto Little Ones in Christ, I Gave You Milk to Drink, Not Meat—I Cor 3:1, 2), we purpose in this book to treat of whatever belongs to the Christian Religion, in such a way as may tend to the instruction of beginners.[2] We have considered that students in this Science have not seldom been hampered by what they have found written by other authors, partly on account of the multipli-

---

[1] "Master" (Latin, *doctor*) means "teacher", not "lord". A "master" of Catholic Truth is its *servant*.

[2] It may shock the reader to discover that the *Summa* was designed for "beginners", but it should encourage beginners to begin it.

Here is how St. Thomas described his *Summa* when explaining why he could not finish it, after he had had a "mystical experience" (the correct description is "infused contemplation"): "I can write no more; compared with what I have seen, all I have written seems to me as straw."

St. Thomas' close friend, Brother Reginald, testified under oath after St. Thomas' death that he had heard a voice from the crucifix in chapel saying to St. Thomas, "You have written well of Me, Thomas. What will you have as your reward?" And he heard Thomas reply, "Only Thyself, Lord." This reply tells us two things: one, why Thomas was *Saint* Thomas; and two, why he called Socrates the greatest philosopher (S.T. III, 42, 4): because, like St. Thomas, Socrates knew he was always a beginner. (See *Apology* 20d–23b.)

37

cation of useless questions, articles, and arguments; partly also because those things that are needful for them to know are not taught according to the order of the subject-matter, but according as the plan of the book might require, or the occasion of the argument offer; partly, too, because frequent repetition brought weariness and confusion to the minds of the readers.

Endeavoring to avoid these and other like faults, we shall try, by God's help, to set forth whatever is included in this Sacred Science as briefly and clearly as the matter itself may allow.[3]

---

[3] Note how St. Thomas practices what he preaches in this Prologue even as he preaches it.

QUESTION I

The Nature and Extent
of Sacred Doctrine

FIRST ARTICLE

*Whether, besides Philosophy, Any Further
Doctrine Is Required?*

Objection 1. It seems that, besides philosophical science,
we have no need of any further knowledge. For man should
not seek to know what is above reason:[1] *Seek not the things
that are too high for thee* (Sir 3:22). But whatever is not above
reason is fully treated of in philosophical science. Therefore
any other knowledge besides philosophical science is superfluous.

Objection 2. Further, knowledge can be concerned only
with being, for nothing can be known, save what is true;
and all that is, is true.[2] But everything that is, is treated of in
philosophical science—even God Himself; so that there is a
part of philosophy called theology,[3] or the divine science, as
Aristotle has proved (*Metaph.* 6). Therefore, besides philosophical science, there is no need of any further knowledge.

On the contrary, It is written (2 Tim 3:16): *All Scripture*[4]
inspired of God is profitable to teach, to reprove, to correct, to in-

---

[1] I.e., more than what can be (a) discovered, (b) understood, or (c)
proved by human reason alone.

[2] Cf. S.T. I, 16, 3.

[3] This is "natural theology" (or "rational theology" or "philosophical theology") as distinct from "revealed theology". It is known by
reason alone, not by faith in divine revelation.

[4] Note how closely St. Thomas' theology is identified with Scripture, its data. ªThe common Protestant objection that this theology is

struct in justice. Now Scripture, inspired of God, is no part of philosophical science, which has been built up by human reason. Therefore it is useful that besides philosophical science there should be other knowledge—*i.e.*, inspired of God.

I answer that, It was necessary for man's salvation[5] that there should be a knowledge revealed by God, besides philosophical science built up by human reason.

Firstly, indeed, because man is directed to God, as to an end that surpasses the grasp of his reason: *The eye hath not seen, O God, besides Thee, what things Thou hast prepared for them that wait for Thee* (Is 66:4). But the end must first be known by men who are to direct their thoughts and actions to the end. Hence it was necessary for the salvation of man that certain truths which exceed human reason should be made known to him by divine revelation.

Even as regards those truths about God which human reason could have discovered, it was necessary that man should be taught by a divine revelation; because the truth about God such as reason could discover, would only be known by a few, and that after a long time, and with the admixture of many errors.[6] Whereas man's whole salvation, which is in God, depends upon the knowledge of this truth. Therefore, in order that the salvation of men might be brought about more fitly and more surely,[7] it was necessary that they should be taught divine truths by divine revelation. It was there-

---

more rationalistic and Greek than believing and biblical is a radical inaccuracy.

[5] Note that although St. Thomas is a theoretical philosopher, and although theology is primarily a theoretical science (S.T. I, 1, 4), St. Thomas sees God's reason for revealing theology's data as primarily a practical one: our salvation.

[6] Cf. St. Thomas' *Summa contra Gentiles* I, 4 for a fuller treatment of this point.

[7] N.b.: this seems to imply that pagans too can be saved, though less "fitly" and "surely".

fore necessary that, besides philosophical science built up by reason there should be a sacred science learned through revelation.

Reply Obj. 1. Although those things which are beyond man's knowledge may not be sought for by man through his reason, nevertheless, once they are revealed by God they must be accepted by faith. Hence the sacred text continues, *For many things are shown to thee above the understanding of man* (Sir 3:25). And in this the sacred science consists.

Reply Obj. 2. Sciences are differentiated according to the various means through which knowledge is obtained. For the astronomer and the physicist both may prove the same conclusion—that the earth, for instance, is round:[8] the astronomer by means of mathematics (*i.e.*, abstracting from matter), but the physicist by means of matter itself. Hence there is no reason why those things which may be learned from philosophical science, so far as they can be known by natural reason, may not also be taught us by another science so far as they fall within revelation. Hence theology included in sacred doctrine differs in kind from that theology which is part of philosophy.

---

[8] N.b.: the Middle Ages did *not* believe the myth of a flat earth; modernity believes the myth of an ignorant Middle Ages.

TENTH ARTICLE

Whether in Holy Scripture a Word May Have Several Senses? [9]

Objection 1. It seems that in Holy Writ a word cannot have several senses, historical or literal, allegorical, tropological or moral, and anagogical. For many different senses in one text produce confusion and deception and destroy all force of argument. Hence no argument, but only fallacies, can be deduced from a multiplicity of propositions. But Holy Writ ought to be able to state the truth without any fallacy. Therefore in it there cannot be several senses to a word.

On the contrary, Gregory says, (*Moral.* xx. 1): *Holy Writ*

---

[9] This article, seemingly out of place, is included here because it concerns the way in which we interpret theology's data, Scripture.

Modern hermeneutics (the science of interpretation) tends to create a great divide between the Modernist Demythologizers, who interpret as merely symbolic whatever passages are too miraculous or supernaturalistic for their philosophy to stomach, and the Fundamentalists, who in reaction to the Modernists tend to be suspicious of all symbolism and confine themselves to literal interpretation of every passage (*except* Jn 6:48−56).

St. Thomas cuts across this either/or and maintains that a passage could rightly be interpreted both literally ("historically") and symbolically ("spiritually"), because God writes history as man writes words. That is, behind this hermeneutic is a metaphysic: the sacramental view of nature and history, according to which things and events as well as words can be *signs* as well as *things*, can be means by which other things are signified and known as well as being things known themselves.

This view of nature and history as signs and not only things, and therefore as objectively *significant*, implicitly presupposes theism; for only God, not man, could be the author of this significance in nature and history which comes to us as given rather than from us as contrived. This sacramental view of nature has been abandoned correctly in modern science (for methodological purposes), unnecessarily in modern philosophy, and disastrously in modern consciousness.

by the manner of its speech transcends every science, because in one and the same sentence, while it describes a fact, it reveals a mystery.

I answer that, The author of Holy Writ is God, in whose power it is to signify His meaning, not by words only (as man also can do), but also by things themselves. So, whereas in every other science things are signified by words, this science has the property, that the things signified by the words have themselves also a signification. Therefore that first signification whereby words signify things belongs to the first sense, the historical or literal. That signification whereby things signified by words have themselves also a signification is called the spiritual sense, which is based on the literal, and presupposes it [A].[10] Now this spiritual sense has a threefold division. For as the Apostle says (Heb 10:1) the Old Law is a figure of the New Law, and Dionysius says (*Coel. Hier.* i) *the New Law itself is a figure of future glory.* Again, in the New Law, whatever our Head has done is a type of what we ought to do. Therefore, so far as the things of the Old Law signify the things of the New Law, there is the allegorical sense; so far as the things done in Christ, or so far as the things which signify Christ, are types of what we ought to do, there is the moral sense. But so far as they signify what relates to eternal glory, there is the anagogical sense.[11] Since the literal sense is that which the author in-

---

[10] These three principles (see Reply to Objection 1 for B and C) prevent the spiritual, symbolic interpretation from becoming uncontrolled and irresponsible. They put a sober and scientific control on this imaginative aspect of interpretation, like putting a strong rider on a strong horse. This imaginative aspect is neglected or scorned today partly because of the false notion that such controls were not known or practiced in medieval theology. Sometimes they were not. But sometimes (as in St. Thomas) they were.

[11] "Old Law" = "Old Testament"; "New Law" = "New Testament"; "future glory" = Heaven. An example of allegorical sense would be Moses (symbolic of Christ) leading the Hebrews (symbolic of the Church, Christ's Body) through the exodus (symbolic of salva-

tends, and since the author of Holy Writ is God, Who by one act comprehends all things by His intellect, it is not unfitting, as Augustine says (*Confess*. xii), if, even according to the literal sense, one word in Holy Writ should have several senses.

Reply Obj. 1. The multiplicity of these senses does not produce equivocation or any other kind of multiplicity, seeing that these senses are not multiplied because one word signifies several things; but because the things signified by the words can be themselves types of other things. Thus in Holy Writ no confusion results, for all the senses are founded on one—the literal—from which alone can any argument be drawn, and not from those intended in allegory [B], as Augustine says (*Epist*. xlviii). Nevertheless, nothing of Holy Scripture perishes on account of this, since nothing necessary to faith is contained under the spiritual sense which is not elsewhere put forward by the Scripture in its literal sense [C]. . . .

---

tion) from slavery (symbolic of sin) to Pharaoh (symbolic of Satan), ruler of Egypt (symbolic of this fallen world), across the Red Sea (symbolic of death), through the wilderness (symbolic of Purgatory), to the Promised Land (symbolic of Heaven). An example of the moral sense would be Christ's washing of His disciples' feet (Jn 13), symbolizing our obligation to serve our neighbors humbly. An example of the anagogical, or eschatological, sense would be Christ's miracles of healing blind men symbolizing His complete healing of our spiritual blindness in Heaven's Beatific Vision.

II. PROOFS FOR
THE EXISTENCE OF GOD

QUESTION 2

The Existence of God

Because the chief aim of sacred doctrine is to teach the knowledge of God, not only as He is in Himself, but also as He is the beginning of things and their last end, and especially of rational creatures, as is clear from what has been already said, therefore, in our endeavor to expound this science, we shall treat: (1) Of God; (2) Of the rational creature's advance towards God; (3) Of Christ, Who as man, is our way to God.

In treating of God there will be a threefold division:

For we shall consider (1) Whatever concerns the Divine Essence; (2) Whatever concerns the distinctions of Persons; (3) Whatever concerns the procession of creatures from Him.

Concerning the Divine Essence, we must consider:

(1) Whether God exists? (2) The manner of His existence, or, rather, what is *not* the manner of His existence; (3) Whatever concerns His operations—namely, His knowledge, will, power.

Concerning the first, there are three points of inquiry:

(1) Whether the proposition "God exists" is self-evident? (2) Whether it is demonstrable? (3) Whether God exists?[1]

---

[1] If the existence of God is self-evident, it is superfluous to try to

FIRST ARTICLE

Whether the Existence of God is Self-Evident?

Objection 1. It seems that the existence of God is self-evident. Now those things are said to be self-evident to us the knowledge of which is naturally implanted in us, as we can see in regard to first principles. But as Damascene says (*De Fid. Orth.* i. 1, 3), *the knowledge of God is naturally implanted in all.*[2] Therefore the existence of God is self-evident.

✻ *Objection 2.*[3] Further, those things [propositions] are said to be self-evident which are known [to be true] as soon as the terms are known [understood], which the Philosopher —Ar (1 *Poster.* iii) says is true of the first principles of demonstration. Thus, when the nature of a whole and a part is known, it is at once recognized that every whole is greater than its part. But as soon as the signification of the word "God" is understood, it is at once seen that God exists. For by this word is signified that thing than which nothing greater can be conceived. But that which exists actually and mentally

---

demonstrate (prove) it. No one *proves* "2 + 2 = 4" or "something exists". In Article 1, St. Thomas shows that God's existence is not so obvious that it needs no proof; and in Article 2 he shows that it is not so obscure that it cannot be proved. Thus he refutes both extremes of "dogmatism" and "skepticism" about the existence of God.

[2] For the vast majority of all humans who have ever lived have believed in some God. Children (or societies) have to be educated out of theism into atheism, not vice versa. Atheism always comes later.

[3] St. Thomas here rephrases St. Anselm's famous "ontological argument" (*Proslogion* chap. 2), interpreting it as an attempt to demonstrate not only that God exists but that God's existence is self-evident, i.e., that the proposition "God exists" is a self-evident proposition, like "Bachelors are males" or "Wholes are greater than their parts". St. Thomas includes St. Anselm's argument as an *objection* to his thesis that the existence of God is *not* self-evident. St. Thomas disagrees with St. Anselm's argument (cf. Reply to Objection), but not, of course, with its conclusion (that God exists).

is greater than that which exists only mentally.[4] Therefore, since as soon as the word "God" is understood it exists mentally, it also follows that it exists actually. Therefore the proposition "God exists" is self-evident.

Objection 3. Further, the existence of truth is self-evident. For whoever denies the existence of truth grants that truth does not exist: and, if truth does not exist, then the proposition "Truth does not exist" is true: and if there is anything true, there must be truth. But God is truth itself: *I am the way, the truth, and the life* (Jn 14:6). Therefore "God exists" is self-evident.

On the contrary, No one can mentally admit the opposite of what is self-evident; as the Philosopher (*Metaph.* iv. lect. vi) states concerning the first principles of demonstration. But the opposite of the proposition "God is" can be mentally admitted: *The fool said in his heart, There is no God* (Ps 52:1). Therefore, that God exists is not self-evident.

✳ *I answer that,* A thing can be self-evident in either of two ways; on the one hand, self-evident in itself, though not to us; on the other, self-evident in itself, and to us.[5] A proposition is self-evident because the predicate is included in the essence of the subject, as "Man is an animal," for animal is contained in the essence of man. If, therefore the essence

---

[4] I.e., "that which exists actually" (objectively, outside man's mind) is a greater concept than "that which exists only mentally" (subjectively, within man's mind). Therefore, "God does not exist" becomes a self-contradictory proposition (and its opposite, "God exists", thus becomes a self-evident proposition). "God lacks existence" means "The greatest conceivable being lacks one conceivable perfection, viz., objective existence."

[5] A proposition that is "self-evident in itself" is one whose predicate is logically identical with or contained in the meaning of its subject. A proposition that is "self-evident to us" must first be self-evident in itself, and it is also self-evident to us if it contains only terms which we can define, by knowing their essences. The following chart may be useful:

of the predicate and subject be known to all, the proposition will be self-evident to all; as is clear with regard to
the first principles of demonstration, the terms of which are
common things that no one is ignorant of, such as being
and non-being, whole and part, and such like. If, however,
there are some to whom the essence of the predicate and
subject is unknown, the proposition will be self-evident in
itself, but not to those who do not know the meaning of
the predicate and subject of the proposition. Therefore, it
happens, as Boëthius says (*Hebdom.*, the title of which is:
"Whether all that is, is good"), "that there are some mental
concepts self-evident only to the learned, as that incorporeal substances are not in space." Therefore I say that this
proposition, "God exists," of itself is self-evident, for the

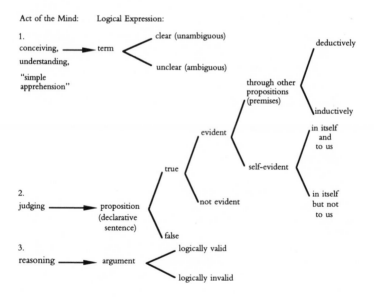

Act of the Mind: Logical Expression:

1.
conceiving, ———▶ term ⟨ clear (unambiguous)
understanding,   unclear (ambiguous)
"simple
apprehension"

                                                                    deductively

                                                through other
                                                propositions
                                                (premises)

                                                                    inductively

                                    evident   in itself
                                                                    and
                                                                    to us

                            true   self-evident

2.
judging ———▶ proposition   not evident   in itself
             (declarative   but not
             sentence)   to us

                            false

3.
reasoning ———▶ argument ⟨ logically valid
                          logically invalid

predicate is the same as the subject; because God is His own existence as will be hereafter shown (Q. 3, A. 4). Now because we do not know the essence of God, the proposition is not self-evident to us; but needs to be demonstrated by things that are more known to us, though less known in their nature[6]—namely, by effects.

✖ *Reply Obj. 1.* To know that God exists in a general and confused way is implanted in us by nature, inasmuch as God is man's beatitude. For man naturally desires happiness, and what is naturally desired by man must be naturally known to him. This, however, is not to know absolutely[7] that God exists; just as to know that someone is approaching is not the same as to know that Peter is approaching, even though it is Peter who is approaching; for many there are who imagine that man's perfect good which is happiness, consists in riches, and others in pleasures, and others in something else.

— *Reply Obj. 2.* Perhaps not everyone who hears this word "God" understands it to signify something than which nothing greater can be thought, seeing that some have believed God to be a body. Yet, granted that everyone understands that by this word "God" is signified something than which nothing greater can be thought, nevertheless, it does not therefore follow that he understands that what the word signifies exists actually, but only that it exists mentally. Nor can it be argued that it actually exists, unless it be admitted that there actually exists something than which nothing

---

[6] I.e., the nature of God is perfectly intelligible, clear, rational, and like light in itself, while the nature of a creature (e.g., a stone) is a mixture of form (which is the intelligible object of knowledge) and matter (which of itself is formless potentiality and is thus not knowable in itself). Yet creatures are more easily known by us than God is, for our minds are proportioned to them more than to God, as the eyes of the owl are proportioned to dim night light, not bright day light.

[7] I.e., explicitly as vs. implicitly and specifically and clearly as vs. "in a general and confused way".

greater can be thought; and this precisely is not admitted by those who hold that God does not exist.[8]

Reply Obj. 3. The existence of truth in general is self-evident but the existence of a Primal Truth is not self-evident to us.

SECOND ARTICLE

Whether It Can Be Demonstrated That God Exists?

Objection 1. It seems that the existence of God cannot be demonstrated. For it is an article of faith that God exists. But what is of faith cannot be demonstrated, because a demonstration produces scientific knowledge; whereas faith is of the unseen (Heb 11:1). Therefore it cannot be demonstrated that God exists.

Objection 2. Further, the essence is the middle term of demonstration.[9] But we cannot know in what God's essence consists, but solely in what it does not consist; as Damascene says (*De Fid. Orth.* i. 4). Therefore we cannot demonstrate that God exists.

Objection 3. Further, if the existence of God were demonstrated, this could only be from His effects. But His effects are not proportionate to Him, since He is infinite and His effects are finite; and between the finite and infinite there is no proportion. Therefore, since a cause cannot be demon-

---

[8] St. Thomas' refutation of St. Anselm's argument here is essentially that it begs the question by implicitly assuming the point to be proved, viz., that there is a referent or denotation (real being) corresponding to the meaning or connotation of the term "that than which nothing greater can be conceived".

[9] A true "demonstration" is not merely any deductive argument, but a proof that a certain property necessarily follows from the essence. Euclid's geometry is full of such demonstrations. "Rational animals are mortal; Socrates is a rational animal; therefore Socrates is mortal" is a demonstration, using "rational animal" as the middle term:

strated by an effect not proportionate to it, it seems that the existence of God cannot be demonstrated.

On the contrary, The Apostle says: *The invisible things of Him are clearly seen, being understood by the things that are made* (Rom 1:20).[10] But this would not be unless the existence of God could be demonstrated through the things that are made; for the first thing we must know of anything is, whether it exists.

→ *I answer that,* Demonstration can be made in two ways: One is through the cause, and is called *a priori,* and this is to argue from what is prior absolutely. The other is through the effect, and is called a demonstration *a posteriori*; this is to argue from what is prior relatively only to us. When an effect is better known to us than its cause, from the effect we proceed to the knowledge of the cause.[11] And from every

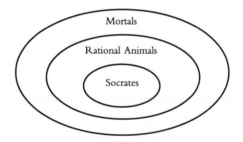

---

[10] Note the irony here: it is sacred Scripture, and faith in it, that says the existence of God is "clearly seen" by natural reason, not just by faith and Scripture.

[11] Demonstration can be either a priori (from the cause as premise to its effect as conclusion) or a posteriori (from the effect as premise to its cause as conclusion). A cause is prior to its effect objectively, in itself ("absolutely"). A premise is prior to the conclusion subjectively, in our knowledge ("relatively to us"). Thus in an a posteriori demonstration,

effect the existence of its proper cause can be demonstrated, so long as its effects are better known to us; because since every effect depends upon its cause, if the effect exists, the cause must pre-exist. Hence the existence of God, in so far as it is not self-evident to us, can be demonstrated from those of His effects which are known to us.

Reply Obj. 1. The existence of God and other like truths about God, which can be known by natural reason, are not articles of faith,[12] but are preambles to the articles; for faith presupposes natural knowledge, even as grace presupposes nature, and perfection supposes something that can be perfected. Nevertheless, there is nothing to prevent a man, who cannot grasp a proof, accepting, as a matter of faith, something which in itself is capable of being scientifically known and demonstrated.

Reply Obj. 2. When the existence of a cause is demonstrated from an effect, this effect takes the place of the definition of the cause in proof of the cause's existence.[13] This is especially the case in regard to God, because, in order to prove the existence of anything, it is necessary to accept as a middle term the meaning of the word, and not its essence,[14] for the question of its essence follows on the question of its

---

that which is posterior in itself (the effect) is prior in our knowledge, as the premise.

[12] I.e., they are not objectively, or in themselves, articles of faith. "Article of faith" is used here in the technical sense.

[13] The definition or essence of the cause is the middle term in an a priori demonstration, e.g., "All animals are mortal, and all men are animals, therefore all men are mortal." "Animal" is part of man's definition (essence) and the cause of man's mortality.

The existence of the effect is the middle term in an a posteriori demonstration, e.g., "Where there are footprints, there were feet, and there are footprints on this beach, therefore there were feet on this beach." Footprints = the middle term here, and is the effect (of feet).

[14] In the example above (n. 13), we need not know the *essence* of footprints for the demonstration to be valid, but we do need to know the meaning of the word.

existence. Now the names given to God are derived from His effects; consequently, in demonstrating the existence of God from His effects, we may take for the middle term the meaning of the word "God."

Reply Obj. 3. From effects not proportionate to the cause no perfect knowledge of that cause can be obtained. Yet from every effect the existence of the cause can be clearly demonstrated, and so we can demonstrate the existence of God from His effects; though from them we cannot perfectly know God as He is in His essence.[15]

THIRD ARTICLE

Whether God Exists?

Objection 1.[16] It seems that God does not exist; because if one of two contraries be infinite, the other would be altogether destroyed. But the word "God" means that He is infinite goodness. If, therefore, God existed, there would be

---

[15] Similarly to n. 14, from knowing a footprint we do not yet know the essence of feet, or have perfect or adequate knowledge of feet. Or, from an artefact we cannot know the essence of the arteficer, but we can know his existence. Note how severely St. Thomas restricts the extent of our rational knowledge of God. He is closer in spirit to agnosticism than to dogmatism.

[16] N.b.: St. Thomas can find only two objections to the existence of God in the whole history of human thought! There are numerous alternative psychological explanations for belief in God (fear, folly, fallacy, or fantasy), and there are objections to each of the many arguments for the existence of God. But there are only two arguments that even claim to *disprove* the existence of God. And the second only claims to show that the existence of God is an unnecessary hypothesis, like the existence of leprechauns or Martians: disappearing Irish gold can be adequately explained without leprechauns, and the "canals" on Mars without Martians. The second Objection does not prove that God cannot possibly exist. Only the first Objection, the Problem of Evil, remains as an apparent *proof* of atheism.

no evil discoverable; but there is evil in the world. Therefore God does not exist.

Objection 2.[17] Further, it is superfluous to suppose that
what can be accounted for by a few principles has been produced by many. But it seems that everything we see in the
world can be accounted for by other principles, supposing
God did not exist. For all natural things can be reduced to
one principle, which is nature; and all voluntary things can
be reduced to one principle, which is human reason, or will.
Therefore there is no need to suppose God's existence.

On the contrary, It is said in the person of God: *I am Who
am* (Ex 3:14).[18]

St. Augustine had two famous formulations of the Problem of Evil
that were similar, and similarly condensed: (1) "If there is God, how
can there be evil? But if there is no God, how can there be good?"
(2) "If God is all-good, He wants His creatures to be happy, and if He
is all-powerful, He can do whatever He wants. But His creatures are
not happy. Therefore He lacks either goodness or power or both." See
C. S. Lewis' *The Problem of Pain* for the best answer to this formulation.

[17] Objection 2 tries to prove, not that God does not exist, but that
the existence of God is like Martians, or Santa Claus, or the conspiracy
theory of history: a hypothesis that is superfluous to a scientific explanation of all the phenomena we observe. Since all five of St. Thomas'
proofs ("ways") begin with sense data and try to prove that a God, or
First Cause, is the only possible adequate rational explanation of this
data, Objection 2 is very serious and relevant to St. Thomas' empirical, scientific arguments. N.b.: medieval science, like modern science,
used the principle of simplicity, or "Ockham's Razor": always prefer
the simpler hypothesis. St. Thomas' objection appeals to this in the
first sentence. But medieval science, unlike modern science, did not
exclude questions (and answers) about first, ultimate causes. Therefore both philosophy and physics come under the heading of "science"
for the Middle Ages, and are not kept strictly separated, as they are in
modern times.

[18] Note the irony and humor here: the "on the contrary" is usually an
argument from authority; so what authority does St. Thomas appeal
to on the question of whether God exists? God Himself! God cuts

→ *I answer that,* The existence of God can be proved in five ways.[19]

to p. 56

---

through our discussion about Him in the third person and announces, in the first person, "I am here!"

[19] Three important notes about the "five ways":

I

These five are not the *proofs* themselves but *ways*, i.e., indications or summaries of proofs. The proofs themselves are elsewhere worked out in much greater detail; e.g., in the *Summa contra Gentiles* the first way takes thirty-one paragraphs (Bk I, chap. 13); here, it takes only one.

II

These five ways are really essentially one way: the "cosmological argument" or argument from the cosmos. The logical structure of all five proofs is the same:

1. There are really three premises:
   a. an implicit logical principle: the tautology that either there is a First Cause or there is not. (The proofs prove there is a First Cause by showing that the alternative entails a contradiction; this presupposes the Law of Excluded Middle: that there can be no middle alternative between two mutually contradictory propositions; thus, to disprove one is to prove the other.)
   b. an explicit empirical datum (motion, causality, etc.)
   c. a metaphysical principle, which is neither tautological, like (a), nor empirical, like (b), but known by metaphysical insight or understanding: e.g., "If there is no First Cause, there can be no second causes", or "nothing can cause itself to be".
2. There are two possible hypotheses to explain the empirical data:
   a. that there is a God (First Mover, Uncaused Cause, etc.)
   b. that there is no God.
   St. Thomas shows in each of the five "ways" that the metaphysical principle (1c) coupled with the empirical data (1b) makes 2b impossible. Thus only 2a is left, if we admit 1a to begin with.
3. However, two "weakening" qualifications must be added:
   a. Each proof individually, and all five together, prove only a

55

thin slice of God, a few attributes of God. More attributes are deduced later in the *Summa*, and much that is known by Revelation is not provable by reason at all (e.g., the Trinity, the Incarnation, and Redemption).

b. Each proof ends with a sentence like "And this is what everyone calls God"—an observation about linguistic usage which answers Pascal's complaint that "the God of the philosophers is not the God of Abraham, Isaac and Jacob" by saying in effect that the God proved here by philosophy, though "thinner" than the God revealed in the Bible, is "thick" enough to refute an atheist. There are simply no other candidates for the position of First Cause, Unmoved Mover, Perfect Being, Cosmic Designer, etc.

III

These five ways are not by any means the only ways of proving the existence of God in the history of philosophy. There have been at least two dozen very different sorts of attempts to prove the existence of God (below). St. Thomas carefully and modestly confines himself to the most scientific proofs alone.

(An Extremely Brief Summary of 24 Arguments for God's Existence)

I. Ontological (Anselm):
   "God" means "that which has all conceivable perfections"; and it is more perfect to exist really than only mentally; therefore God exists really. The most perfect conceivable being cannot lack any conceivable perfection.

II. Cosmological
   A. Motion: Since no thing (or series of things) can move (change) itself, there must be a first, Unmoved Mover, source of all motion.
   B. Efficient Causality: Nothing can cause its own existence. If there is no first, uncaused cause of the chain of causes and effects we see, these second causes could not exist. They do, so It must.

C. Contingency and Necessity: Contingent being (beings able not to be) depend on a Necessary Being (a being not able not to be).

D. Degrees of Perfection: Real degrees of real perfections presuppose the existence of that perfection itself (the Perfect Being).

E. Design: Design can be caused only by an intelligent Designer. Mindless nature cannot design itself or come about by chance.

F. The *Kalam* (Time) Argument: Time must have a beginning, a first moment (creation) to give rise to all other moments. (The "Big Bang" seems to confirm this: time had an absolute beginning fifteen to twenty billion years ago.) And the act of creation presupposes a Creator.

III. Psychological
   A. from mind and truth
      1. Augustine: Our minds are in contact with eternal, objective, and absolute truth superior to our minds (e.g. $2 + 2 = 4$), and the eternal is divine, not human.
      2. Descartes: Our *idea* of a perfect being (God) could not have come from any imperfect source (cause), for the effect cannot be greater than the cause. Thus it must have come from God.
   B. from will and good
      1. Kant: Morality requires a perfect ideal, and requires that this ideal be actual and real, somewhere.
      2. Newman: Conscience speaks with absolute authority, which could come only from God.
   C. from emotions and desire
      1. C. S. Lewis: Innate desires correspond to real objects, and we have an innate desire (at least unconsciously) for God, and Heaven.
      2. Von Balthasar: Beauty reveals God. There is Mozart, therefore there must be God.
   D. from experience
      1. Existential Argument: If there is no God (and no immortality) life is ultimately meaningless.
      2. Mystical experience meets God.

The first and more manifest[20] way is the argument from motion. It is certain, and evident to our senses, that in the

---

3. Ordinary religious experience (prayer) meets God. (Prayer of the Skeptic: "God, if you exist, show me" —a real experiment.)

4. Love argument: If there is no God of Love, no Absolute that is love, then love is not absolute. Or, the eyes of love reveal the infinite value of the human person as the image of God.

IV. The argument from the analogy of other minds, which are no harder to prove than God (Plantinga).

V. The practical argument: Pascal's Wager: To bet on God is your only chance of winning eternal happiness, and to bet against Him is your only chance of losing. It is the most reasonable bet in life.

VI. Historical

A. from miracles: If miracles exist, a supernatural miracle-worker exists.

B. from Providence, perceivable in history (e.g., in Scripture) and in one's own life.

C. from authority: Most good, wise, reliable people believe in God.

D. from saints: You see God through them. Where do they get their joy and power?

E. from Jesus: If God is unreal, Jesus was history's biggest fool or fake.

(This list is not exhaustive, but illustrative. Maritain and Marcel, for example, have formulated other, more complex arguments for God.)

[20] St. Thomas is not saying that the first of the five ways is easier to follow logically (in fact it is more complex than any of the other four), but that its premise, or data is the most obvious data. This is *motion*, i.e., not just locomotion (motion through space), but any change. Each of the five ways begins with a different datum (motion, causality, possibility, degrees of perfection, and order) and arrives at the same conclusion: God, under five different attributes: Prime Mover, Uncaused Cause, Necessary Being, Most Perfect Being, Ordering Mind.

world some things are in motion. Now whatever is in motion is put in motion by another, for nothing can be in motion except it is in potentiality to that towards which it is in motion; whereas a thing moves inasmuch as it is in act. For motion is nothing else than the reduction of something from potentiality to actuality. But nothing can be reduced from potentiality to actuality, except by something in a state of actuality. Thus that which is actually hot, as fire, makes wood, which is potentially hot, to be actually hot, and thereby moves and changes it. Now it is not possible that the same thing should be at once in actuality and potentiality in the same respect, but only in different respects. For what is actually hot cannot simultaneously be potentially hot; but it is simultaneously potentially cold. It is therefore impossible that in the same respect and in the same way a thing should be both mover and moved, *i.e.*, that it should move itself. Therefore, whatever is in motion must be put in motion by another. If that by which it is put in motion be itself put in motion, then this also must needs be put in motion by another, and that by another again. But this cannot go on to infinity, because then there would be no first mover, and, consequently, no other mover; seeing that subsequent movers move only inasmuch as they are put in motion by the first mover; as the staff moves only because it is put in motion by the hand. Therefore it is necessary to arrive at a <u>first mover</u>, put in motion by no other; and this everyone understands to be God.[21]

---

[21] The difficult half of this proof is the first half, which proves the commonsensical proposition: "Whatever is in motion, must be put in motion by another." The second half of the proof, which then proves that there can be no infinite regress in movers, is a simple syllogism: If there is no first (un-moved) mover, then there can be no second (moved) movers; but there are second movers; therefore there is a First Mover (cf. *Summa contra Gentiles* I, 13 for an expanded version of this whole argument).

Infinite *progress* in *effects* is possible without contradiction, but infi-

The second way is from the nature of the efficient cause.[22] In the world of sense we find there is an order of efficient causes. There is no case known (neither is it, indeed, possible) in which a thing is found to be the efficient cause of

---

nite *regress* in *causes* is not. For that would be like a train composed of an infinite number of boxcars all moving uphill without a locomotive, or like a stairway with an infinite number of steps each resting on the one below it but with no first step. "Infinite regress" means *indefinite* regress, without a term, or first step. It does not mean a positive, actual infinity like God's attributes.

And "first" in this proof does not necessarily mean first in *time*, only in causality. Sometimes a cause comes temporally before its effect, as parents are born before their children, and the bat swings before the ball is hit; but at other times, the cause and effect are simultaneous, as when the stories of a building, or rungs on a ladder, or books in a pile each rest on the one below it. There too, there must be a first cause (the bottom story, rung, or book *causes* the others to stand), though it is not prior in time.

St. Thomas believed, of course (because he read it in Genesis), that God was prior in time to the universe—not in the sense that God is *in* time or that time existed before the universe existed (like Einstein and unlike Newton, St. Thomas regarded time not as an absolute, prior background to the universe but as co-created with the universe; for him, as for Einstein, time was relative to matter and motion, i.e., to the universe, not vice versa), but in the sense that there is no infinite regress of time, but only a finite regress of time: the universe has existed for only a finite time. (This fact has recently been confirmed by astrophysics in the form of the "Big Bang" as vs. the "Steady State" and "Oscillating" models of the universe.) But St. Thomas did not think that philosophical reason without divine revelation could prove the universe had only a finite time span, as the "kalam" (time) argument used by some medieval Muslim and Christian philosophers tried to prove, because God *could* have created a universe with infinite time, co-eternal with Himself. That is not *logically* impossible, and therefore cannot be logically disproved. The universe is finite in time only because God's free will chose to create it that way.

[22] "Efficient cause" for Aristotle meant only "cause of *change*, cause of form informing matter". But for St. Thomas it means also the cause of the very *existence* of its effect. Thus the second way goes beyond

itself; for so it would be prior to itself, which is impossible. Now in efficient causes it is not possible to go on to infinity, because in all efficient causes following in order, the first is the cause of the intermediate cause, and the intermediate is the cause of the ultimate cause, whether the intermediate cause be several, or one only. Now to take away the cause is to take away the effect. Therefore, if there be no first cause among efficient causes, there will be no ultimate, nor any intermediate cause. But if in efficient causes it is possible to go on to infinity, there will be no first efficient cause, neither will there be an ultimate effect, nor any intermediate efficient causes; all of which is plainly false. Therefore it is necessary to admit a first efficient cause, to which everyone gives the name of God.

The third way is taken from possibility and necessity, and runs thus. We find in nature things that are possible to be and not to be,[23] since they are found to be generated, and to corrupt, and consequently, they are possible to be and not to be. But it is impossible for these always to exist, for that which is possible not to be at some time is not.[24]

---

the first: the first proved God as cause of universal change; the second proves God as cause of the very existence of the universe.

The argument here is similar to that in the last half of the first way: if no First (Uncaused) Cause, no second causes; but there are second causes; therefore there is a First Cause. "Infinite regress" is impossible because it means "no First Cause".

[23] "Things that are possible to be and not to be" = "things whose existence is contingent", "things that have a potentiality to not-be as well as to be", "things that can go out of existence or fail to come into existence". "Generation" = "coming into existence"; "corruption" = "going out of existence".

[24] I.e., given infinite time, every possibility is eventually actualized. N.b.: this proof, like the others, is a *reductio ad absurdum*, which examines the hypothesis of atheism (no God, no Necessary Being) and perceives that this hypothesis logically entails a conclusion which is evidently false (thus the hypothesis must be false), viz., that nothing exists now. For if there has been infinite time (which there must have

Therefore, if everything is possible not to be, then at one time there could have been nothing in existence. Now if this were true, even now there would be nothing in existence, because that which does not exist only begins to exist by something already existing. Therefore, if at one time nothing was in existence, it would have been impossible for anything to have begun to exist; and thus even now nothing would be in existence—which is absurd. Therefore, not all beings are merely possible, but there must exist something the existence of which is necessary.

But every necessary thing[25] either has its necessity caused by another, or not. Now it is impossible to go on to infinity in necessary things which have their necessity caused by another, as has been already proved in regard to efficient causes. Therefore we cannot but postulate the existence of some being having of itself its own necessity, and not receiving it from another, but rather causing in others their necessity. This all men speak of as God.

The fourth way is taken from the gradation to be found in things.[26] Among beings there are some more and some less good, true, noble, and the like. But "more" and "less" are predicated of different things, according as they resemble in their different ways something which is the maximum, as a thing is said to be hotter according as it more nearly resembles that which is hottest; so that there is some-

---

been if there is no Creator), then every possibility must have already had enough time to have been actualized, including the possibility of simultaneous nonexistence for all contingent beings.

[25] The last half of the proof, which speaks of a plurality of necessary beings, refers to changeless angels (in biblical terms) or bodiless "intelligences" (in Aristotelian terms).

[26] The fourth way presupposes something which everyone except a few Sophists in ancient Greece and Skeptics in ancient Rome accepted until modern times, and which the modern mind tends to find incomprehensible: viz., that "values" are objective, that value judgments are judgments of fact—e.g., that a man *really* has more value than an ape.

thing which is truest, something best, something noblest, and, consequently, something which is uttermost being; for those things that are greatest in truth are greatest in being, as it is written in *Metaph.* ii.[27] Now the maximum in any genus is the cause of all in that genus; as fire, which is the maximum of heat, is the cause of all hot things. Therefore there must also be something which is to all beings the cause of their being, goodness, and every other perfection; and this we call God.[28]

The fifth way is taken from the governance of the world. We see that things which lack intelligence, such as natural bodies, act for an end, and this is evident from their acting always, or nearly always, in the same way, so as to obtain the best result. Hence it is plain that not fortuitously, but designedly, do they achieve their end. Now whatever lacks intelligence cannot move towards an end, unless it be directed by some being endowed with knowledge and intelligence; as the arrow is shot to its mark by the archer. Therefore some intelligent being exists by whom all natural things are directed to their end; and this being we call God.[29]

---

[27] The concept of degrees of being as well as of goodness, and of an "uttermost being" as well as a "greatest good", will probably seem very strange to the modern reader. But a thing must first *be* before it can be good (thus whatever has goodness must also have being), and every thing that has being also has some goodness (cf. S.T. I, 5, 3); therefore goodness and being are coextensive. The concept of degrees of being can be understood if we remember that "being" means not simply existence ("to be or not to be") but also essence (*what* a thing is, its nature), and this latter aspect of being admits of degrees.

[28] The point of the argument is that "better" implies "best". Put dynamically, progress presupposes an unchanging standard to judge the progress. If the standard also progressed, how could we progress to it? How could we reach or even approach a goal line that moved with us?

St. Thomas' example of this principle (fire) is, of course, bad science. But the invalid illustration does not invalidate the principle.

[29] This is often called the "argument from design". It is probably the most popular and instinctively obvious of all arguments for the

Reply Obj. 1. As Augustine says (*Enchir.* xi): *Since God is the highest good, He would not allow any evil to exist in His works, unless His omnipotence and goodness were such as to bring good even out of evil.* This is part of the infinite goodness of God, that He should allow evil to exist, and out of it produce good.[30]

Reply Obj. 2. Since nature works for a determinate end under the direction of a higher agent, whatever is done by nature must needs be traced back to God, as to its first cause. So also whatever is done voluntarily must also be traced back to some higher cause other than human reason or will, since these can change and fail; for all things that are changeable and capable of defect must be traced back to an immovable and self-necessary first principle, as was shown in the body of the *Article.*[31]

---

existence of God. As Paley said, if we find a watch, it is reasonable to conclude there is a watchmaker.

[30] Like Scripture, St. Augustine and St. Thomas answer the problem of evil not with some timeless formula but with a dramatic promise for the future: since evil occurs in history, its solution also occurs in history. The greatest example in history of both evil and of God producing good from it is the Crucifixion.

[31] The natural and human sciences of themselves need not raise questions of ultimate origin. But philosophy must. Once the philosophical question is raised of the ultimate origin of the data of the natural and human sciences, the five ways prove that God is the only adequate answer to that question.

III. THE NATURE OF GOD

QUESTION 3

Of the Simplicity of God

When the existence of a thing has been ascertained there remains the further question of the manner of its existence, in order that we may know its essence.[1] Now, because we cannot know what God is, but rather what He is not, we have no means for considering how God is, but rather how He is not.[2]

Therefore, we must consider (1) How He is not; (2) How He is known by us; (3) How He is named.[3]

---

[1] N.b.: for St. Thomas "essence" = ultimately "manner (mode, way) of existence". Essence is relative to existence, as potency to act. Existence (*esse*) is the ultimate actuality and is therefore also the nature (essence) of God. In Him alone essence and existence are identical.

[2] Note how scrupulously St. Thomas confines our knowledge of God and how fruitfully he develops that knowledge within those bounds. Cf. S.T. I, 13, 5: we must choose between positive but analogical knowledge of God (what God is *like*, not what He *is*) or univocal but negative knowledge of God (what He is *not*).

[3] N.b.: these three questions correspond to the three meanings of *logos* in the Greek language and Greek philosophy: (1) intelligible being, (2) intelligence, and (3) communication; or (1) essence, (2) concept, and (3) word. Gorgias the Sophist formulated a philosophy of total skepticism with his three theses that (1) there is no Being (i.e., intelligible being, *logos*), (2) if there were, we could not have knowledge (*logos*) of it, and (3) if we could know it, we could not have communication (*logos*) of it. The history of Western philosophy has also passed through three corresponding stages: (1) the ancient and medieval period, which concentrated on metaphysics (being), (2) the classical modern period,

Now it can be shown how God is not, by denying of Him whatever is opposed to the idea of Him—viz., composition, motion, and the like. Therefore (1) we must discuss His simplicity,[4] whereby we deny composition in Him; and because whatever is simple in material things is imperfect and a part of something else, we shall discuss (2) His perfection; (3) His infinity; (4) His immutability; (5) His unity.

Concerning His simplicity, there are eight points of inquiry: (1) Whether God is a body? (2) Whether He is composed of matter and form? (3) Whether in Him there is composition of quiddity, essence or nature, and subject? (4) Whether He is composed of essence and existence? (5) Whether He is composed of genus and difference? (6) Whether He is composed of subject and accident? (7) Whether He is in any way composite, or wholly simple? (8) Whether He enters into composition with other things?

---

which concentrated on epistemology (knowledge), and (3) the contemporary period, which concentrates on philosophy of language and communication of meaning.

[4] St. Thomas deduces many other (negative) attributes of God from the one attribute of simplicity (noncomposedness), for there are many kinds of composition to be denied (see next paragraph).

In *this* (footnoted) paragraph, note that divine attributes 2−5 are all negative to our understanding, though positive in themselves. Our idea of God's perfection, infinity, immutability, and unity is negative because it comes from our experience of imperfection, finitude, temporality, and plurality: we deny that these apply to God. We do not have a positive understanding of God's perfection, infinity, immutability, and unity.

SEVENTH ARTICLE

Whether God Is Altogether Simple?

Objection 2. . . . Whatever is best must be attributed to God. But with us that which is composite is better than that which is simple; thus, chemical compounds are better than simple elements, and animals than the parts that compose them. Therefore it cannot be said that God is altogether simple. . . .

I answer that, The absolute simplicity of God may be shown in many ways. First, from the previous articles of this question. For there is neither composition of quantitative parts in God, since He is not a body; nor composition of form and matter; nor does His nature differ from His *suppositum* [person-substance]; nor His essence from His existence; neither is there in Him composition of genus and difference, nor of subject and accident. Therefore, it is clear that God is nowise composite, but is altogether simple.[5]

Secondly, because every composite is posterior to its component parts, and is dependent on them; but God is the first being, as shown above (Q. 2, A. 3).

Thirdly, because every composite has a cause, for things in themselves different cannot unite unless something causes them to unite. But God is uncaused, as shown above (*loc. cit.*), since He is the first efficient cause.

Fourthly, because in every composite there must be potentiality and actuality; but this does not apply to God; for either one of the parts actuates another, or at least all the parts are potential to the whole. . . .

Reply Obj. 2. With us composite things are better than simple things, because the perfections of created goodness

---

[5] This is an inductive argument by complete enumeration. Each of the six kinds of composition cannot exist in God, therefore no composition can exist in God.

cannot be found in one simple thing, but in many things. But the perfection of divine goodness is found in one simple thing (QQ. 4, A. 1, and 6, A. 2).

The Existence of God in Things[6]

FIRST ARTICLE

Whether God Is in All Things?

Objection 1. It seems that God is not in all things. For what is above all things is not in all things. But God is above all, according to the Psalm (112:4), *The Lord is high above all nations*, etc. Therefore God is not in all things.[7]

Objection 2. Further, what is in anything is thereby contained. Now God is not contained by things, but rather does He contain them. Therefore God is not in things; but things are rather in Him. Hence Augustine says (*Octog. Tri. Quaest.*, qu. 20), that *in Him things are, rather than He is in any place.*

Objection 3. Further, the more powerful an agent is, the more extended is its action. But God is the most powerful of all agents. Therefore His action can extend to things which are far removed from Him; nor is it necessary that He should be in all things.

Objection 4. Further, the demons are beings. But God is not in the demons; for there is no fellowship between light and darkness (2 Cor 6:14). Therefore God is not in all things.

On the contrary, A thing is wherever it operates.[8] But God operates in all things, according to Isaiah 26:12, *Lord . . .*

---

[6] The previous question explored God's transcendence and difference from all things: Christianity is not pantheism. This question explores God's *presence* in all things: Christianity is not deism either.

[7] Objection 1 assumes, in effect (in the second sentence) that deism and pantheism are the only two possibilities, because it works within sensory-imaginative categories of "inside" and "outside" (or "above"). The Reply interprets these two prepositions metaphysically rather than physically. The same is true of Objection and Reply 2.

[8] We, too! Our being is not confined to our skin—that is epidermi-

Thou hast wrought all our works in [Vulg., *for*] *us.* Therefore God is in all things.

I answer that, God is in all things; not, indeed, as part of their essence, nor as an accident; but as an agent is present to that upon which it works. For an agent must be joined to that wherein it acts immediately, and touch it by its power; hence it is proved in *Physic.* vii that the thing moved and the mover must be joined together. Now since God is very being by His own essence, created being must be His proper effect; as to ignite is the proper effect of fire. Now God causes this effect in things not only when they first begin to be, but as long as they are preserved in being;[9] as light is caused in the air by the sun as long as the air remains illuminated. Therefore as long as a thing has being, God must be present to it, according to its mode of being. But being is innermost in each thing and most fundamentally inherent in all things since it is formal [actual] in respect of everything found in a thing, as was shown above (Q. 7, A. 1). Hence it must be that God is in all things, and innermostly.[10]

---

olatry, idolatry of the epidermis—but is like a magnetic field. The footnoted sentence is the essence of Einstein's Field Theory of matter too, as vs. Newton's notion of matter as existing only inside its surface boundaries. Einstein defined a physical body as existing wherever it produced an effect.

[9] This sharply distinguishes Christianity from deism. A carpenter does not cause the very being of the house he builds, only its form; therefore when he stops working, the house continues to exist. But if God stopped "working" (cf. Jn 5:17), the very existence of all things would perish, for this is His work.

[10] Gilson calls this "the Great Syllogism":

   1. Being is innermost in each thing;

   2. But God is Being (His essence is existence);

   3. Therefore God is innermost in each thing.

Nothing is more inner, present, and intimate to every being than God. God activates every being from within, so to speak. N.b.: God can be thus supremely present and immanent only because He is supremely transcendent, i.e., He is pure, infinite existence, not existence limited

Reply Obj. 1. God is above all things by the excellence of His nature; nevertheless, He is in all things as the cause of the being of all things; as was shown above in this article.

Reply Obj. 2. Although corporeal things are said to be in another as in that which contains them, nevertheless spiritual things contain those things in which they are; as the soul contains the body.[11] Hence also God is in things as containing them: nevertheless by a certain similitude to corporeal things, it is said that all things are in God; inasmuch as they are contained by Him.

Reply Obj. 3. No action of an agent, however powerful it may be, acts at a distance, except through a medium. But it belongs to the great power of God that He acts immediately in all things. Hence nothing is distant from Him, as if it could be without God in itself. But things are said to be distant from God by the unlikeness to Him in nature or grace; as also He is above all by the excellence of His own nature.[12]

Reply Obj. 4. In the demons there is their nature which is from God, and also the deformity of sin which is not from

---

by a finite essence. If He were one of many essences, He could not be present in opposite essences. Blue cannot be present in red because it is a different essence, but colorless light can be present in red and blue and all colors. God (and existence) is like light in this analogy. Cf. also Article 2.

[11] A remote physical analogy might be the sea being "in" a sunken ship. St. Thomas' analogy is better: the body is *in* the soul rather than vice versa, as we usually think. (How materialistic our usual thinking is!) Even Descartes was victimized by this sensory-imaginative picture-thinking when he struggled with the mind-body problem. He thought, for a time, that the soul might be "in" the pineal gland! And we still often think the mind is "in" the brain. That is like thinking a computer programmer is "in" his hardware. He transcends even his software, how much more his hardware!

[12] God is transcendent in *nature*, not in *place*. He is here, now, present to this place and time and to all places and times. God is transcendent in His *nature* and immanent in His *presence*.

Him; therefore, it is not to be absolutely conceded that God is in the demons, except with the addition, *inasmuch as they are beings*. But in things not deformed in their nature, we must say absolutely that God is.

The Immutability of God

FIRST ARTICLE

Whether God Is Altogether Immutable?

Objection 3. . . . To approach and to recede signify movement. But these are said of God in Scripture, *Draw nigh to God, and He will draw nigh to you* (James 4:8). Therefore God is mutable.[13]

On the contrary, It is written, *I am the Lord, and I change not* (Mal 3:6).

I answer that, From what precedes, it is shown that God is altogether immutable.

First, because it was shown above that there is some first being, whom we call God; and that this first being must be pure act, without the admixture of any potentiality, for the reason that, absolutely, potentiality is posterior to act. Now everything which is in any way changed, is in some way in potentiality. Hence it is evident that it is impossible for God to be in any way changeable.

Secondly, because everything which is moved, remains as it was in part, and passes away in part; as what is moved from whiteness to blackness, remains the same as to substance; thus in everything which is moved, there is some kind of composition to be found. But it has been shown above (Q. 3, A. 7) that in God there is no composition,

---

[13] The main *religious* argument for modern "process theology" is that a mutable and changing God is necessary to theologically ground the experienced changing relationship with God that this verse designates. It is alleged that an immutable God would make such a real, lived relationship of change impossible.

for He is altogether simple. Hence it is manifest that God cannot be moved.

Thirdly, because everything which is moved acquires something by its movement, and attains to what it had not attained previously. But since God is infinite, comprehending in Himself all the plenitude of perfection of all being, He cannot acquire anything new, nor extend Himself to anything whereto He was not extended previously. Hence movement in no way belongs to Him.[14]. . .

Reply Obj. 3. These things are said of God in Scripture metaphorically. For as the sun is said to enter a house, or to go out, according as its rays reach the house, so God is said to approach to us, or to recede from us, when we receive the influx of His goodness, or decline from Him.[15]

---

[14] As usual, the only recourse for one who would deny the conclusion (God's immutability) is to deny the premise (that God is actual, one, and infinite, not potential, compound, or finite).

[15] Thus the experience of a changing *relationship* is accounted for.

QUESTION 13

The Names of God

*Whether What Is Said of God and of Creatures
Is Univocally Predicated of Them?*

On the contrary, Whatever is predicated of various things
under the same name but not in the same sense, is predicated equivocally.[16] But no name belongs to God in the
same sense that it belongs to creatures; for instance, wisdom in creatures is a quality, but not in God.[17] Now a different genus changes an essence, since the genus is part of
the definition; and the same applies to other things. Therefore whatever is said of God and of creatures is predicated
equivocally.

---

[16] If St. Thomas held that terms could be univocally predicated of
God and creatures (i.e., mean the same thing when used to describe
God and creatures, as predicates), he would have an anthropomorphic
conception of God and a rationalistic conception of the human mind.
If he held that all terms predicated of God and creatures were equivocal, he would be agnostic about God and skeptical about the human
mind. Analogical predication fits between these two popular extremes.
Univocal terms about God are negative, and positive terms about God
are analogical.

"Equivocal" is used in this Article in a broad sense, meaning simply
not-univocal. "Equivocal" here can include "analogical". Later, in the
body of this Article, he uses "equivocal" in a narrower sense as distinct
from "analogical" as well as from "univocal".

[17] The attributes of God are not accidents, qualities added to His
substance. God *is* His wisdom, and truth, and righteousness, etc. Cf.
Jn 11:25; 14:6. Therefore although "wise" in "that man is wise" is in
the genus *quality*, "wise" in "God is wise" is not. If it were in any
genus, it would be substance, for everything in God is His substance
or essence.

Further, God is more distant from creatures than any creatures are from each other. But the distance of some creatures makes any univocal predication of them impossible, as in the case of those things which are not in the same genus. Therefore much less can anything be predicated univocally of God and creatures; and so only equivocal predication can be applied to them.[18]

I answer that, . . . as said in the preceding article, all perfections existing in creatures divided and multiplied, pre-exist in God unitedly. Thus, when any term expressing perfection is applied to a creature, it signifies that perfection distinct in idea from other perfections; as, for instance, by this term *wise* applied to a man, we signify some perfection distinct from a man's essence, and distinct from his power and existence, and from all similar things; whereas when we apply it to God, we do not mean to signify anything distinct from His essence, or power, or existence. Thus also this term *wise* applied to man in some degree circumscribes and comprehends the thing signified; whereas this is not the case when it is applied to God; but it leaves the thing signified as incomprehended;[19] and as exceeding the signification of the name. Hence it is evident that this term *wise* is not applied in the same way to God and to man. The same rule applies to other terms. Hence no name is predicated univocally of God and of creatures.

Neither, on the other hand, are names applied to God and creatures in a purely equivocal sense, as some have said. Because if that were so, it follows that from creatures nothing

---

[18] Compare the meaning of "good" in "good doggie", "good man", and "good God". The goodness of a man is closer to the goodness of a dog, even though the dog lacks reason and morality, than to the goodness of God; for any two finite things are closer to each other than either is to the infinite.

[19] "Uncomprehended" does not mean "totally unknown" but "not surrounded or controlled", not *adequately* known. Cf. I, 12, 7, Reply 1 for what St. Thomas means by "comprehension".

could be known or demonstrated about God at all; for the reasoning would always be exposed to the fallacy of equivocation. Such a view is against the philosophers, who proved many things about God, and also against what the Apostle says: *The invisible things of God are clearly seen being understood by the things that are made* (Rom 1:20). Therefore it must be said that these names are said of God and creatures in an analogous sense, that is, according to proportion.[20]

Now names are thus [analogously] used in two ways: either according as many things are proportionate to one, thus for example *healthy* is predicated of medicine and urine in relation and in proportion to health of a body, of which the former is the sign and the latter the cause: or according as one thing is proportionate to another, thus *healthy* is said of medicine and animal, since medicine is the cause of health in the animal body. And in this way some things are said of God and creatures analogically, and not in a purely equivocal nor in a purely univocal sense. For we can name God only from creatures (A. 1). Thus, whatever is said of God and creatures, is said according to the relation of a creature to God as its principle and cause, wherein all perfections of things pre-exist excellently. Now this mode of community of idea is a mean between pure equivocation and simple univocation. For in analogies the idea is not, as it is in univocals, one and the same, yet it is not totally diverse as in equivocals.[21] . . .

---

[20] I.e., wisdom in God is infinite and one with God's essence because it is proportionate to God's being, which is infinite and one with His essence; while wisdom in man is finite and distinct from his essence because it is proportionate to man's being, which is finite and composed of essence plus existence.

[21] Thus, to summarize, all names of God and all terms predicable of God designate either (1) God's essence (Being, existence, I AM WHO AM), (2) what God is *not* (univocal negative terms like "eternal" [not-temporal] and "immaterial"), (3) what God is *like* (analogical positive terms like "wise" and "good"), (4) *relationships* to God (e.g.,

QUESTION 14

Of God's Knowledge

Whether God Knows Things Other Than Himself?[22]

Objection 2. . . . The object understood is the perfection of the one who understands. If therefore God understands other things besides Himself, something else will be the perfection of God, and will be nobler than He; which is impossible.

Objection 3. . . . The act of understanding is specified [determined] by the intelligible object, as is every other act from its own object. Hence the intellectual act is so much the nobler, the nobler the object understood. But God is His own intellectual act. If therefore God understands anything other than Himself, then God Himself is specified [determined] by something else than Himself; which cannot be. Therefore He does not understand things other than Himself.

"Creator", "Lord", "Redeemer"), or (5) mere metaphors ("Rock", "Lion").

[22] The issue is critical for the Middle Ages, since Aristotle, who seemed to be speaking for reason, contradicted faith and divine revelation here. Aristotle taught that God, being perfect, knew only that object perfectly worth knowing, viz., Himself, and did not know or love or providentially care for things other than Himself. To preserve the synthesis of faith and reason and show the reasonableness of the Christian faith, St. Thomas had to show Aristotle's rational mistake here. In the body of the article St. Thomas validates God's knowledge of objects other than Himself without compromising His perfection or unity or lowering Him to the human, subject-object mode of knowing, by appealing again, as he does so often, to the fact of *creation*.

On the contrary, It is written: *All things are naked and open to His eyes* (Heb 4:13).

I answer that, God necessarily knows things other than Himself. For it is manifest that He perfectly understands Himself; otherwise His existence would not be perfect, since His existence is His act of understanding. Now if anything is perfectly known, it follows of necessity that its power is perfectly known. But the power of anything can be perfectly known only by knowing to what its power extends. Since therefore the divine power extends to other things by the very fact that it is the first effective cause of all things, as is clear from the aforesaid (Q. 2, A. 3), God must necessarily know things other than Himself. . . .

Reply Obj. 2. The object understood is a perfection of the one understanding not by its substance, but by its image, according to which it is in the intellect, as its form and perfection, as is said in *De Anima* iii. For *a stone is not in the soul, but its image.* Now those things which are other than God are understood by God, inasmuch as the essence of God contains their images as above explained; hence it does not follow that there is any perfection in the divine intellect other than the divine essence.

Reply Obj. 3. The intellectual act is . . . specified . . . by the principal object understood in which other things are understood. . . . This . . . in God is nothing but His own essence in which all images of things are comprehended. Hence it does not follow that the divine intellectual act, or rather God Himself, is specified by anything else than the divine essence itself.

EIGHTH ARTICLE

Whether the Knowledge of God Is the Cause of Things?

On the contrary, Augustine says (*De Trin.* xv), *Not because they are, does God know all creatures spiritual and temporal, but because He knows them, therefore they are.*[23]

I answer that, The knowledge of God is the cause of things. For the knowledge of God is to all creatures what the knowledge of the artificer is to things made by his art. Now the knowledge of the artificer is the cause of the things made by his art, . . . [but] the intelligible form does not denote a principle of action in so far as it resides in the one who understands unless there is added to it the inclination to an effect, which inclination is through the will. . . .

Reply Obj. 3. Natural things are midway between the knowledge of God and our knowledge: for we receive knowledge from natural things, of which God is the cause by His knowledge. Hence, as the natural objects of knowledge are prior to our knowledge, and are its measure, so, the knowledge of God is prior to natural things, and is the measure of them; as, for instance, a house is midway between the knowledge of the builder who made it, and the knowledge of the one who gathers his knowledge of the house from the house already built.[24]

---

[23] Cf. Ps 1:6. The "Copernican revolution" of Kantian epistemology (man's mind imposing form rather than discovering it), and, even more, the epistemology of his successor Fichte, in which the mind (ego) creates (posits) the matter as well as the form, is quite incorrect for man but quite correct for God.

[24] Cf. 16, 1. A whole world view is implied here. It seems human science as reading God's art (for "God wrote two books, nature and scripture", according to the medieval maxim). This view was as habitual and natural to medieval man as the positivistic-materialistic-empiricistic-

QUESTION 16

Of Truth

EIGHTH ARTICLE

Whether Truth Is Immutable?[25]

I answer that, Truth, properly speaking, resides only in the intellect, as said before (A. 1); but things are called true in virtue of the truth residing in an intellect. Hence the mutability of truth must be regarded from the point of view of the intellect. . . . If, then, there is an intellect wherein there can be no alternation of opinions, and the knowledge of which nothing can escape, in this is immutable truth. Now such is the divine intellect, as is clear from what has been

---

scientific-secular world view is to modern man. The medieval world view includes, surrounds, and expands the modern one:

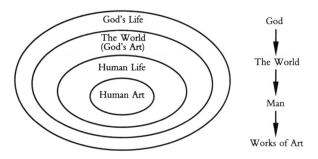

In these two diagrams, both the arrows and the enclosing circles represent the relationship of determining, forming, or making. The lower level, or smaller circle, is relative to the higher or larger one.

[25] St. Thomas here argues from the eternity of the divine intellect to the eternity of truth. Augustine argued from the eternity of truth to the existence of an eternal divine intellect.

said before (Q. 14, A. 15). Hence the truth of the divine intellect is immutable. But the truth of our intellect is mutable; not because it is itself the subject of change, but in so far as our intellect changes from truth to falsity.[26]. . .

---

[26] N.b.: even the truth *we* know ("objective truth") is not a changing *truth* if it is a truth about unchanging things, like "justice is a virtue" or "$2+2=4$", rather than about changing things like "Caesar crossed the Rubicon"; but our *knowledge* of it is a changing *knowledge* or opinion ("subjective truth").

QUESTION 19

The Will of God

FIFTH ARTICLE

*Whether Any Cause Can Be Assigned
to the Divine Will?*

Objection 1. It seems that some cause can be assigned to
the divine will. For Augustine says (Qq. lxxxiii. 46): *Who
would venture to say that God made all things irrationally?* But
to a voluntary agent, what is the reason of operating, is the
cause of willing. Therefore the will of God has some cause.[27]

Objection 2. . . . If . . . there is no cause of His will, we
cannot seek in any natural things any cause, except the divine will alone. Thus all science would be in vain. . . .

I answer that, In no wise has the will of God a cause. In
proof of which we must consider that, since the will follows
from the intellect, there is a cause of the will in the person
that wills, in the same way as there is a cause of the understanding, in the person that understands. The case with the
understanding is this: that if the premiss and its conclusion
are understood separately from each other, the understanding of the premiss is the cause that the conclusion is known.
If the understanding perceive the conclusion in the premiss
itself, apprehending both the one and the other at the same
glance, in this case the knowing of the conclusion would
not be caused by understanding the premises, since a thing

---

[27] Cf. Socrates' question in the *Euthyphro*: "Is a thing pious because
the gods love it, or do the gods love it because it is pious?" The problem is to avoid both the intellectual imperfection of arbitrariness (the
first alternative in Socrates' question) and the volitional imperfection of
God's will being formed, determined, and judged by anything outside
Himself (Socrates' second alternative).

cannot be its own cause; and yet, it would be true that the thinker would understand the premises to be the cause of the conclusion. It is the same with the will, with respect to which the end stands in the same relation to the means to the end, as do the premises to the conclusion with regard to the understanding.

Hence, if anyone in one act wills an end, and in another act the means to that end, his willing the end will be the cause of his willing the means. This cannot be the case if in one act he wills both end and means; for a thing cannot be its own cause. Yet it will be true to say that he wills to order to the end the means to the end. Now as God by one act understands all things in His essence, so by one act He wills all things in His goodness. Hence, as in God to understand the cause is not the cause of His understanding the effect, for He understands the effect in the cause, so, in Him, to will an end is not the cause of His willing the means, yet He wills the ordering of the means to the end. Therefore, He wills this to be as means to that; but does not will this on account of that.[28]

Reply Obj. 1. The will of God is reasonable, not because anything is to God a cause of willing, but in so far as He wills one thing to be on account of another.

Reply Obj. 2. . . . God wills effects to proceed from definite causes, for the preservation of order in the universe. . . .

---

[28] It may help to think of the analogy of a human novelist conceiving and willing, all at once, the entire plot of his novel, *in* which perfect order demands that one event take place because of and after another.

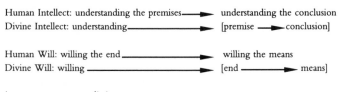

Human Intellect: understanding the premises——▶ understanding the conclusion
Divine Intellect: understanding——————▶ [premise ——▶ conclusion]

Human Will: willing the end——————▶ willing the means
Divine Will: willing ——————————▶ [end ————————▶ means]

(arrows represent causality)

QUESTION 20

God's Love

SECOND ARTICLE

Whether God Loves All Things?

Objection 4. . . . It is written (Ps 5:7): *Thou hatest all the workers of iniquity.* Now nothing is at the same time hated and loved. Therefore God does not love all things.

On the contrary, It is said (Wis 11:25): *Thou lovest all things that are, and hatest none of the things which Thou hast made.*

I answer that, God loves all existing things. For all existing things, in so far as they exist, are good, since the existence of a thing is itself a good; and likewise, whatever perfection it possesses. Now it has been shown above (Q. 19, A. 4) that God's will is the cause of all things. It must needs be, therefore, that a thing has existence, or any kind of good, only inasmuch as it is willed by God. To every existing thing, then, God wills some good. Hence, since to love anything is nothing else than to will good to that thing, it is manifest that God loves everything that exists. Yet not as we love. Because since our will is not the [active] cause of the goodness of things, but is [passively] moved by it as by its object, our love, whereby we will good to anything, is not the cause of its goodness; but conversely its goodness, whether real or imaginary, calls forth our love, by which we will that it should preserve the good it has, and receive besides the good it has not, and to this end we direct our actions: whereas the love of God infuses and creates goodness.[29]. . .

---

[29] For God is pure act, without potentiality, and therefore without being caused or moved (changed) by other things. God does not fall in love for the same reason water does not get wet.

Reply Obj. 4. Nothing prevents one and the same thing being loved under one aspect, while it is hated under another. God loves sinners in so far as they are existing natures; for they have existence, and have it from Him. In so far as they are sinners, they have not existence at all, but fall short of it; and this in them is not from God. Hence under this aspect, they are hated by Him.[30]

THIRD ARTICLE

Whether God Loves All Things Equally?

On the contrary, Augustine says (*Tract. in Joan.* cx): *God loves* [1] *all things that He has made, and amongst them* [2] *rational creatures more, and of these especially* [3] *those who are members of his only-begotten Son; and much more than all,* [4] *His only-begotten Son Himself.*

I answer that, Since to love a thing is to will it good, in a twofold way anything may be loved more, or less. In one way on the part of the act of the will itself, which is more or less intense. In this way God does not love some things more than others, because He loves all things by an act of the will that is one, simple, and always the same. In another way on the part of the good itself that a person wills for the beloved. In this way we are said to love that one more than another, for whom we will a greater good, though our will is not more intense. In this way we must needs say that God loves some things more than others. For since God's love

---

[30] God practices what He preaches to us: love the sinner and hate the sin. God loves even the being He created in the devil, but not the lack of being in the devil's sin. St. Thomas is not saying that sinners have no existence, but that they lack the fullness of existence that comes from loving the good. Vice and virtue have an ontological dimension as well as a moral one; we diminish our being when we sin and augment it by the virtues.

is the cause of goodness in things, as has been said (A. 2), no one thing would be better than another, if God did not will greater good for one than for another.[31] . . .

---

[31] It may shock those whose real religion is Americanism, but God is not an American. God's love is hierarchically ordered, as ours should be. (Does anyone really think we should love people no more than animals?) The argument in the last sentence of the Article seems simple and decisive.

The Providence of God

FOURTH ARTICLE

Whether Providence Imposes Any Necessity on Things Foreseen?

Objection 1. It seems that divine providence imposes necessity upon things foreseen . . . for divine providence cannot be frustrated.[32]. . .

On the contrary, Dionysius says that (*Div. Nom.* iv. 23) *to corrupt nature is not the work of providence.* But it is in the nature of some things to be contingent. Divine providence does not therefore impose any necessity upon things so as to destroy their contingency.

I answer that, Divine providence imposes necessity upon some things; not upon all, as some formerly believed. For to providence it belongs to order things towards an end. Now after the divine goodness, which is an extrinsic end to all things, the principal good in things themselves is the perfection of the universe; which would not be, were not all grades of being found in things. Whence it pertains to divine providence to produce every grade of being. And thus it has prepared for some things necessary causes, so that they happen of necessity; for others contingent causes, that they

---

[32] St. Thomas answers the objection not by compromising the efficacy or infallibility of divine providence at all, but by deriving from it (and from the principle that grace perfects nature rather than corrupting it) the proper contingency of human events. (Cf. I, 19, 8.) Essentially, the objection is that because God's will is never frustrated, therefore all effects are necessary; and the answer is that precisely because God's will is never frustrated, therefore not all effects are necessary.

may happen by contingency, according to the nature of their proximate causes.

Reply Obj. 1. The effect of divine providence is not only that things should happen somehow; but that they should happen either by necessity or by contingency. Therefore whatsoever divine providence ordains to happen infallibly and of necessity happens infallibly and of necessity; and that happens from contingency, which the plan of divine providence conceives to happen from contingency. . . .

IV. COSMOLOGY:
CREATION AND PROVIDENCE

❧

QUESTION 46

Of the Beginning of
the Duration of Creatures

FIRST ARTICLE

Whether the Universe of Creatures Always Existed? [1]

Objection 1. It would seem that the universe of creatures, called the world, had no beginning, but existed from eternity. For everything which begins to exist, is a possible be-

---

[1] The issue is important for the Middle Ages because Aristotle had apparently proved that the world was eternal, but Scripture had revealed that it had a beginning; thus philosophy and revealed theology, reason and faith, seemed to contradict each other, invalidating the central medieval enterprise of their marriage.

In modern scientific cosmology, the "Steady State theory" was the equivalent of the Aristotelian eternal universe theory, and the "Big Bang" theory, which gives the world a temporal beginning, fits in nicely with the idea of creation *of* time (rather than creation *in* time). The scientific evidence seems to have refuted the "Steady State" and confirmed the "Big Bang" pretty conclusively, thus also confirming once again that faith and reason never really contradict each other.

N.b.: Article 1 shows that we cannot prove that the world is eternal; Article 2 shows that we cannot prove by philosophy alone that it is not. Philosophical reasoning leaves both options as logical possibilities. Divine revelation (and today perhaps also scientific data) resolve the question; philosophy does not.

ing before it exists: otherwise it would be impossible for it to exist. If therefore the world began to exist, it was a possible being before it began to exist. But possible being is matter. . . . If therefore the world began to exist, matter must have existed before the world. . . .

Objection 3. Further, what is unbegotten has no beginning. But the Philosopher (*Phys.* i, text. 82) proves that matter is unbegotten, and also (*De Coelo et Mundo* i, text. 20) that the heaven [the firmament, "the heavens"] is unbegotten. Therefore the universe did not begin to exist.

Objection 4. Further, a vacuum is where there is not a body, but there might be. But if the world began to exist, there was first no body where the body of the world now is; and yet it could be there, otherwise it would not be there now. Therefore before the world there was a vacuum; which is impossible.[2]

Objection 5. Further, nothing begins anew to be moved except through being otherwise than it was before. . . . What is otherwise now than it was before, is moved. Therefore before every new movement there was a previous movement. Therefore movement always was;[3] and therefore also the thing moved always was, because movement is only in a movable thing.

Objection 6. . . . He who wills to make a house tomorrow, and not today, awaits something which will be tomorrow,

---

[2] It was a supposed truism of medieval physics that a vacuum is impossible.

[3] This is an argument of Aristotle (*Physics*, Bk. 8) for the eternity of the world. St. Thomas answers it in the Reply by distinguishing *creation* (of existence) from *change* (of state)—a distinction Aristotle did not use, for, not knowing that the world was created, he never wondered why it *existed* but took its existence for granted and wondered only about its *nature* and properties. The doctrine of creation, as an answer to a question the Greeks did not ask, led Christian philosophers to ask the new question, and thus to become aware of the distinction between existence and essence.

but is not today; and at least awaits for today to pass, and for tomorrow to come; and this cannot be without change.[4]. . . Therefore before every new movement, there was a previous movement; and so the same conclusion follows as before. . . .

I answer that, Nothing except God can be eternal. And this statement is far from impossible to uphold: for it has been shown above (Q. 19, A. 4) that the will of God is the cause of things. Therefore things are necessary, according as it is necessary for God to will them, since the necessity of the effect depends on the necessity of the cause (*Metaph.* v, text. 6). Now it was shown above (Q. 19, A. 3), that, absolutely speaking, it is not necessary that God should will anything except Himself. It is not therefore necessary for God to will that the world should always exist; but the world exists forasmuch as God wills it to exist, since the being of the world depends on the will of God, as on its cause. It is not therefore necessary for the world to be always; and hence it cannot be proved by demonstration.

Nor are Aristotle's reasons (*Phys.* viii) simply, but relatively, demonstrative—viz., in order to contradict the reasons of some of the ancients who asserted that the world began to exist in some quite impossible manner. This appears in three ways. Firstly, because both in *Phys.* viii and in *De Coelo* i, text. 101, he premises some opinions, as those of Anaxagoras, Empedocles and Plato, and brings forward reasons to refute them. Secondly, because wherever he speaks

---

[4] This is similar to the question, Why did God create the world eighteen billion years ago, and not at some other time? What was He doing before He created? The reply is (1) that there *is* no "before creation" since time itself is a creature, and (2) the distinction between (a) an eternal will to create a temporal world, (b) an eternal will to create an eternal world, and (c) a temporal will to create a temporal world. The objector's question assumes that (c) is the truth, since the world is temporal. Aristotle would be closest to (b), minus "creation". St. Thomas teaches (a).

of this subject, he quotes the testimony of the ancients, which is not the way of a demonstrator, but of one persuading of what is probable. Thirdly, because he expressly says (*Topic.* i. 9), that there are dialectical problems, about which we have nothing to say from reason, as, *whether the world is eternal.*

Reply Obj. 1. Before the world existed it was possible for the world to be, not, indeed, according to a passive power which is matter, but according to the active power of God. . . .

Reply Obj. 3. Aristotle (*Phys.* i, text. 82) proves that matter is unbegotten from the fact that it has not a subject from which to derive its existence;[5] and (*De Coelo et Mundo* i, text. 20) he proves that heaven ["the heavens"] is ungenerated, forasmuch as it has no contrary from which to be generated. Hence it appears that no conclusion follows either way, except that matter and heaven did not begin by generation, as some said, especially about heaven. But we say that matter and heaven were produced into being by creation, as appears above (Q. 44, A. 1 *ad* 2).

Reply Obj. 4. The notion of a vacuum is not only *in which is nothing*, but also implies a space capable of holding a body and in which there is not a body, as appears from Aristotle (*Phys.* iv, text. 60). Whereas we hold that there was no place or space before the world was.

Reply Obj. 5. The first mover was always in the same state: but the first movable thing was not always so, because it began to be whereas hitherto it was not. This, however, was not through change, but by creation, which is not change, as said above (Q. 45, A. 2 *ad* 2). . . .

Reply Obj. 6. The first agent is a voluntary agent. And although He had the eternal will to produce some effect,

---

[5] This is *unimaginable*, for imagination requires space and time. A vacuum is imaginable, however. Thus we tend to think mistakenly of "nothing" as a vacuum, i.e., empty space, which is really *something*.

yet He did not produce an eternal effect. . . . But the universal agent who produces the thing and time also, is not correctly described as acting now, and not before, according to an imaginary succession of time succeeding time, as if time were presupposed to His action. . . .

SECOND ARTICLE

Whether It Is an Article of Faith [6]
That the World Began?

Objection 1. It would seem that it is not an article of faith but a demonstrable conclusion that the world began. For everything that is made has a beginning of its duration. But it can be proved demonstratively that God is the effective cause of the world; indeed this is asserted by the more approved philosophers. Therefore it can be demonstratively proved that the world began. . . .

Objection 3. Further, everything which works by intellect, works from some principle [beginning], as appears in all kinds of craftsmen. But God acts by intellect: therefore His work has a principle. The world, therefore, which is His effect, did not always exist. . . .

Objection 6. Further, if the world always was, the consequence is that infinite days preceded this present day. But it is impossible to pass . . . through an infinite medium. Therefore we should never have arrived at this present day; which is manifestly false.[7] . . .

---

[6] I.e., discoverable only by faith, not by unaided reason. After showing, in Article 1, that reason cannot *disprove* the doctrine of the creation of a world with a finite rather than an infinite time span, St. Thomas now shows that reason cannot *prove* it either. The first Article refutes the Latin Averroists; the second refutes the Augustinians.

[7] This is the *kalam* (time) argument used by many medieval Mus-

Objection 8. Further, if the world and generation always were, there have been an infinite number of men. But man's soul is immortal: therefore an infinite number of human souls would actually now exist, which is impossible. Therefore it can be known with certainty that the world began, and not only is it known by faith. . . .

I answer that, By faith alone do we hold, and by no demonstration can it be proved, that the world did not always exist, as was said above of the mystery of the Trinity (Q. 32, A. 1).

The reason of this is that the newness of the world cannot be demonstrated [1] on the part of the world itself. For the principle of demonstration is the essence of a thing. Now everything according to its species [essence] is abstracted from *here* and *now*. . . . Hence it cannot be demonstrated that man, or heaven, or a stone were not always.

Likewise neither can it be demonstrated [2] on the part of the efficient cause, which acts by will. For the will of God cannot be investigated by reason, except as regards those things which God must will of necessity; and what He wills about creatures is not among these, as was said above (Q. 19, A. 3). But the divine will can be manifested by revelation, on which faith rests. Hence that the world began to exist is an object of faith, but not of demonstration or science.

And it is useful to consider this, lest anyone, presuming to demonstrate what is of faith, should bring forward reasons that are not cogent, so as to give occasion to unbelievers to laugh, thinking that on such grounds we believe things that are of faith.[8]

---

lim philosophers and taken over by Christian philosophers like St. Bonaventura.

[8] St. Thomas' tendency is always to be more critical, skeptical, and agnostic rather than credulous. He would rather give no argument than a weak one. This severe habit is often annoying to believers, but the opposite habit is often annoying to unbelievers.

Reply Obj. 1. As Augustine says (*De Civ. Dei* xi. 4), the opinion of philosophers who asserted the eternity of the world was twofold. For some said that the substance of the world was not from God, which is an intolerable error; and therefore it is refuted by proofs that are cogent.[9] Some, however, said that the world was eternal, although made by God. For they hold that the world has a beginning, not of time, but of creation, so that in a certain hardly intelligible way it was always made. And they try to explain their meaning thus (*De Civ. Dei* x. 31): *for as, if the foot were always in the dust from eternity, there would always be a footprint which without doubt was caused by him who trod on it, so also the world always was, because its Maker always existed.* To understand this we must consider that the efficient cause, which acts by motion, of necessity precedes its effect in time. . . . But if the action is instantaneous and not successive, it is not necessary for the maker to be prior to the thing made in duration, as appears in the case of illumination. Hence they say that it does not follow necessarily if God is the active cause of the world, that He should be prior to the world in duration; because creation, by which He produced the world, is not a successive change, as was said above (Q. 45, A. 2).[10] . . .

---

[9] Cf. I, 44, 1.

[10] Distinguish three kinds of efficient causes in regard to time:

1. The most usual kind precede their effects in time. E.g., the bat hitting the ball (the cause) occurs before the ball flies to the outfield (the effect).

2. Sometimes the cause and effect are simultaneous in duration. E.g., an iron ball making an impression in a pillow, or the act of thinking producing an idea in the mind.

3. With regard to the unique kind of efficient cause that is *creating*, the cause and effect can be simultaneous *and* instantaneous rather than durational, since creation is not a process in time (see I, 45, 2). This is impossible for us to imagine, since our image-making faculty can only imagine something in space and time; and it is difficult for us to con-

Reply Obj. 3. This is the argument of Anaxagoras (as quoted in *Phys.* viii, text. 15). But it does not lead to a necessary conclusion, except as to that intellect which deliberates in order to find out what should be done, which is like movement. Such is the human intellect, but not the divine intellect (Q. 14, AA. 7, 12). . . .

Reply Obj. 6. Passage is always understood as being from term to term. Whatever bygone day we choose, from it to the present day there is a finite number of days which can be passed through. The objection is founded on the idea that, given two extremes, there is an infinite number of mean terms.[11]. . .

Reply Obj. 8. Those who hold the eternity of the world evade this reason in many ways. . . . One might say that the world was eternal, or at least some creature, as an angel, but not man. But we are considering the question in general, as to whether any creature can exist from eternity. . . .

---

ceive, but it is barely possible, or "hardly intelligible", as St. Thomas says. It is intelligible at least negatively, through what it is not.

[11] Cf. Zeno's famous paradoxes against motion, which assert the impossibility of passing through an infinite number of points in space in a finite time. The *kalam* argument makes a similar mistake, according to St. Thomas, in asserting the impossibility of passing through an infinite number of days in time. His point is that there *is* no actually infinite number of days, no matter how far back we think. The false premise common to both Zeno's paradoxes and the *kalam* argument is smoked out in the last sentence.

V. ANTHROPOLOGY:
BODY AND SOUL

QUESTION 75

Of Man Who Is Composed of a Spiritual and a Corporeal Substance: and in the First Place, concerning What Belongs to the Essence of the Soul

SIXTH ARTICLE

Whether the Human Soul Is Incorruptible?

Objection 1. It would seem that the human soul is corruptible. For those things that have a like beginning and process seemingly have a like end. But the beginning, by generation, of men is like that of animals, for they are made from the earth. And the process of life is alike in both; because *all things breathe alike, and man hath nothing more than the beast,* as it is written (Qo 3:19). Therefore, as the same text concludes, *the death of man and beast is one, and the condition of both is equal.* But the souls of brute animals are corruptible. Therefore, also, the human soul is corruptible. . . .

I answer that, We must assert that the intellectual principle which we call the human soul is incorruptible. For a thing may be corrupted in two ways—*per se* [by itself] and accidentally. Now it is impossible for any substance to be generated or corrupted accidentally, that is, by the generation or corruption of something else. For generation and corruption belong to a thing, just as existence belongs to it, which is acquired by generation and lost by corruption. Therefore, whatever has existence *per se* cannot be generated or corrupted except *per se*;[1] while things which do not subsist, such as accidents and material forms, acquire existence or lose it through the generation or corruption of composite things. Now it was shown above (AA. 2, 3) that the souls of brutes are not self-subsistent, whereas the human soul is; so that the souls of brutes are corrupted, when their bodies are corrupted; while the human soul could not be corrupted unless it were corrupted *per se*.

This, indeed, is impossible, not only as regards the human soul, but also as regards anything subsistent that is a form alone [without matter]. For . . . it is impossible for a form to be separated from itself; and therefore it is impossible for a subsistent form to cease to exist.[2]

. . . Moreover we may take a sign of this from the fact that everything naturally aspires to existence after its own manner. Now, in things that have knowledge, desire ensues upon knowledge. The senses indeed do not know existence, except under the conditions of *here* and *now*, whereas the intellect apprehends existence absolutely, and for all time; so that everything that has an intellect naturally desires always

---

[1] I.e., whatever has its own act of existence (i.e., whatever is a substance rather than an accident). Accidents (like the whiteness of a seagull) and merely material forms (like the nature of a seagull) can be generated or corrupted by the generation or corruption of the substance in which they inhere (the actual seagull); but a substance (e.g., one seagull) is not generated or corrupted by the generation or corruption of another substance (another seagull).

[2] Corruption takes place by a form being separated from its matter (e.g., the soul being separated from its body). This man, this composite matter-form substance, is corruptible. But the soul, as a form without matter, is not corruptible thus.

to exist. But a natural desire cannot be in vain.[3] Therefore every intellectual substance is incorruptible.

Reply Obj. 1. Solomon reasons thus in the person of the foolish, as expressed in the words of Wisdom 2. Therefore the saying that man and animals have a like beginning in generation is true of the body; for all animals alike are made of earth. But it is not true of the soul. For the souls of brutes are produced by some power of the body; whereas the human soul is produced by God. To signify this, it is written as to other animals: *Let the earth bring forth the living soul* (Gen 1:24): while of man it is written *(ibid.* 2:7) that *He breathed into his face the breath of life.*[4] And so in the last chapter of Ecclesiastes (12:7) it is concluded: *(Before) the dust return into its earth from whence it was; and the spirit return to God Who gave it.* Again the process of life is alike as to the body, concerning which it is written (Qo 3:19): *All things breathe alike,* and (Wis 2:2), *The breath in our nostrils is smoke.* But the process is not alike of the soul; for man is intelligent, whereas animals are not. Hence it is false to say: *Man has nothing more than beasts.* Thus death comes to both alike as to the body, but not as to the soul. . . .

---

[3] St. Thomas was too natural, healthy, and sane to consider seriously the possibility that some people might not share this desire to exist. He was also too natural, healthy, and sane to consider seriously the possibility that the universe is fundamentally meaningless, that it produces in us desires which correspond to no real possible satisfaction at all. No one has ever seen nature producing desires for nonexistent objects. The empirical evidence for "no natural desire is in vain" is 100 percent, and the evidence for its contrary is 0 percent (consider all known natural desires: to eat, drink, sleep, wake, live, walk, copulate, socialize, know, love, be loved, etc.).

[4] This is the fundamental ontological basis for human dignity, intrinsic value, and moral responsibility, viz., the human soul is God-given, not slime-evolved, and its nature is spiritual ("made in the image of God"). Bodies could have evolved, but not souls.

SEVENTH ARTICLE

Whether the Soul Is of the Same Species As an Angel?[5]

Objection 3. Further, it seems that the soul does not differ from an angel except in its union with the body. But as the body is outside the essence of the soul, it seems that it does not belong to its species. Therefore the soul and angel are of the same species.

On the contrary, Things which have different natural operations are of different species. But the natural operations of the soul and of an angel are different; since, as Dionysius says (*Div. Nom.* vii), *Angelic minds have simple and blessed intelligence, not gathering their knowledge of Divine things from visible things.* Subsequently he says the contrary to this of the soul. Therefore the soul and an angel are not of the same species. . . .

Reply Obj. 3. The body is not of the essence of the soul; but the soul by the nature of its essence can be united to the body, so that, properly speaking, not the soul alone, but the *composite*, is the species. And the very fact that the soul in a certain way requires the body for its operation, proves that the soul is endowed with a grade of intellectuality inferior to that of an angel, who is not united to a body.

---

[5] It is a strangely popular notion that after death we become angels. This change of species is, of course, impossible. For one thing, there is a resurrection of the body. For another, even the temporarily disembodied soul, after bodily death and before the general resurrection at the end of time, is a spirit of a different species than an angel, for two reasons: (1) as St. Thomas notes here, human souls know by sensation and reasoning, while angels are purely intuitive; and (2) human souls are essentially forms of bodies, and therefore incomplete without their bodies, while angels have no tendency to inform bodies.

QUESTION 76

Of the Union of Body and Soul

FIFTH ARTICLE

Whether the Intellectual Soul Is Properly United to Such a Body?

Objection 1. It would seem that the intellectual soul is improperly united to such a body. For matter must be proportionate to the form. But the intellectual soul is incorruptible. Therefore it is not properly united to a corruptible body. . . .

Objection 4. Further, what is susceptible of a more perfect form should itself be more perfect. But the intellectual soul is the most perfect of souls. Therefore since the bodies of other animals are naturally provided with a covering, for instance, with hair instead of clothes, and hoofs instead of shoes; and are, moreover, naturally provided with arms, as claws, teeth, and horns; it seems that the intellectual soul should not have been united to a body which is imperfect as being deprived of the above means of protection.

On the contrary, The Philosopher says (*De anima* ii. 1), that *the soul is the act of a physical organic body having life potentially.*

I answer that, Since the form is not for the matter, but rather the matter for the form, we must gather from the form the reason why the matter is such as it is; and not conversely.[6] Now the intellectual soul, as we have seen above (Q. 55, A. 2) in the order of nature, holds the lowest place

---

[6] This principle—explaining matter by form, explaining empirical details by unifying purpose, explaining the lower and lesser by the higher and greater—perhaps better than any one other single notion distinguishes the classical and medieval notion of reason and expla-

among intellectual substances; inasmuch as it is not naturally gifted with the knowledge of truth, as the angels are; but has to gather knowledge from individual things by way of the senses, as Dionysius says (*Div. Nom.* vii). But nature never fails in necessary things: therefore the intellectual soul had to be endowed not only with the power of understanding, but also with the power of feeling. Now the action of the senses is not performed without a corporeal instrument. Therefore it behooved the intellectual soul to be united to a body fitted to be a convenient organ of sense. . . .

Reply Obj. 1. Perhaps someone might attempt to answer this by saying that before sin the human body was incorruptible. This answer does not seem sufficient; because before sin the human body was immortal not by nature, but by a gift of Divine grace; otherwise its immortality would not be forfeited through sin, as neither was the immortality of the devil.[7]

Therefore we answer otherwise by observing that in matter two conditions are to be found; one which is chosen in order that the matter be suitable to the form; the other which follows by force of the first disposition. The artisan, for in-

---

nation from the modern, which tends to the opposite, i.e., to reductionism (e.g., thought is *only* cerebral biochemistry, love is *only* lust, man is *only* a clever ape, etc.). Modern reductionism really begins in the fourteenth century with "Ockham's Razor" and Ockham's most important application of that principle, viz., Nominalism, the doctrine that universality is *only* linguistic, not real; that only names (*nomina*), not forms, are universal.

St. Thomas here explains the union of body and soul from the viewpoint of the needs of the soul, since the body is for the soul, not vice versa, and it is to be explained in terms of the soul, not vice versa, as the setting of a play is explained in terms of its theme, not vice versa.

[7] A good example of how a deductive argument without empirical evidence can still be reasonable. (The skeptic will ask how we could ever know whether the human body before the Fall was mortal, immortal by nature, or immortal by grace.)

stance, for the form of the saw chooses iron adapted for cutting through hard material; but that the teeth of the saw may become blunt and rusted, follows by force of the matter itself. So the intellectual soul requires a body of equable complexion, which, however, is corruptible by force of its matter. If, however, it be said that God could avoid this, we answer that in the formation of natural things we do not consider what God might do; but what is suitable to the nature of things, as Augustine says (*Gen. ad lit.* ii. 1). God, however, provided in this case by applying a remedy against death in the gift of grace. . . .

Reply Obj. 4. The intellectual soul as comprehending universals, has a power extending to the infinite; therefore it cannot be limited by nature to certain fixed natural notions, or even to certain fixed means whether of defence or of clothing, as is the case with other animals, the souls of which are endowed with knowledge and power in regard to fixed particular things. Instead of all these, man has by nature his reason and his hands, which are *the organs of organs* (*De Anima* iii), since by their means man can make for himself instruments of an infinite variety, and for any number of purposes. . . .

VI. EPISTEMOLOGY
AND PSYCHOLOGY

QUESTION 82

Of the Will

THIRD ARTICLE

Whether the Will Is a Higher Power Than the Intellect? [1]

Objection 1. It would seem that the will is a higher power than the intellect. For the object of the will is good and the end. But the end is the first and highest cause. Therefore the will is the first and highest power.

Objection 2. Further, in the order of natural things we observe a progress from imperfect things to perfect. And this also appears in the powers of the soul: for sense precedes the intellect, which is more noble. Now the act of the will, in the natural order, follows the act of the intellect. Therefore the will is a more noble and perfect power than the intellect.

---

[1] This issue, and the one in the following article, is crucial for the enterprise of a marriage of pagan Greek philosophy with Judeo-Christian biblical revelation, for there seems to be a major contradiction here in that for Plato and Aristotle the central, deepest, and highest part of a man is his mind and its knowledge, while in the Bible it is the heart, or will, and its love which are primary. Cf. William Barrett, *Irrational Man*, chap. 4, "Hebraism and Hellenism". St. Thomas, in his usual careful and balanced way, compromises neither insight, but synthesizes them by perceiving a crucial distinction (in the body of this article).

Objection 3. Further, habits are proportioned to their powers, as perfections [are proportioned] to what they make perfect. But the habit which perfects the will—namely, charity —is more noble than the habits which perfect the intellect: for it is written (1 Cor 13:2): *If I should know all mysteries, and if I should have all faith, and have not charity, I am nothing.* Therefore the will is a higher power than the intellect.

On the contrary, The Philosopher holds the intellect to be the highest power of the soul (*Ethic.* x. 7).

I answer that, The superiority of one thing over another can be considered in two ways: *absolutely* and *relatively*. Now a thing is considered to be such absolutely which is considered such in itself: but relatively as it is such with regard to something else. If therefore the intellect and will be considered with regard to themselves, then the intellect is the higher power. And this is clear if we compare their respective objects to one another. For the object of the intellect is more simple and more absolute than the object of the will; since the object of the intellect is the very idea [essence, form] of appetible [desirable] good; and the appetible good, the idea of which is in the intellect, is the object of the will. Now the more simple and the more abstract [immaterial] a thing is, the nobler and higher it is in itself;[2] and therefore the object of the intellect is higher than the object of the will. Therefore, since the proper nature of a power is in its order to its object, it follows that the intellect in itself and absolutely is higher and nobler than the will. But relatively and by comparison with something else, we find that the will is sometimes higher than the intellect, from the fact that the object of the will occurs in something higher than that in

---

[2] This is because it more closely resembles God, the standard of perfection. St. Thomas' point may be put this way: the intellect thinks God's very thoughts after Him, however imperfectly, while the will desires the good *things* of which these thoughts are the archetypes and models.

which occurs the object of the intellect. Thus for instance, I might say that hearing is relatively nobler than sight, inasmuch as something in which there is sound is nobler than something in which there is color, though color is nobler and simpler than sound. For, as we have said above (Q. 16, A. 1; Q. 27, A. 4), the action of the intellect consists in this —that the idea [form] of the thing understood is in the one who understands; while the act of the will consists in this —that the will is inclined to the thing itself as existing in itself. And therefore the Philosopher says in *Metaph*. vi (Did. v. 2) that *good and evil*, which are objects of the will, *are in things*, but *truth and error*, which are objects of the intellect, *are in the mind*.[3] When, therefore, the thing in which there is good is nobler than the soul itself, in which is the idea understood; by comparison with such a thing, the will is higher than the intellect. But when the thing which is good is less noble than the soul, then even in comparison with that thing the intellect is higher than the will. Wherefore the love of God is better than the knowledge of God; but, on the contrary, the knowledge of corporeal things is better than the love thereof.[4] Absolutely, however, the intellect is nobler than the will.

Reply Obj. 1. The aspect of causality is perceived by comparing one thing to another, and in such a comparison the idea of good is found to be nobler: but truth signifies something more absolute, and extends to the idea of good itself: wherefore even good is something true. But, again, truth is something good: forasmuch as the intellect is a thing, and truth its end. And among other ends this is the most excellent:[5] as also is the intellect among the other powers.

---

[3] This does not mean that truth is subjective: cf. S.T. I, 16.

[4] This is the practical "bottom line". It is better to love God than to know God, but it is better to know material things than to love them.

[5] Therefore St. Thomas elsewhere says that the greatest good one can do to his neighbor is to lead him to the truth.

Reply Obj. 2. What precedes in order of generation and time is less perfect: for in one and the same thing potentiality precedes act, and imperfection precedes perfection. But what precedes absolutely and in the order of nature is more perfect: for thus act precedes potentiality. And in this way the intellect precedes the will, as the motive power precedes the thing movable, and as the active precedes the passive; for good which is understood moves the will.

Reply Obj. 3. This reason is verified of the will as compared with what is above the soul. For charity is the virtue by which we love God.

QUESTION 83

Of Free-Will

FIRST ARTICLE

Whether Man Has Free-Will?

Objection 1. It would seem that man has not free-will. For whoever has free-will does what he wills. But man does not what he wills; for it is written (Rom 7:19): *For the good which I will I do not, but the evil which I will not, that I do.* Therefore man has not free-will.

Objection 2. Further, whoever has free-will has in his power to will or not to will, to do or not to do. But this is not in man's power: for it is written (Rom 9:16): *It is not of him that willeth*—namely, to will—*nor of him that runneth*—namely, to run. Therefore man has not free-will.

Objection 3. Further, what is *free is cause of itself*, as the Philosopher says (*Metaph.* i. 2). Therefore what is moved by another is not free. But God moves the will, for it is written (Prov 21:1): *The heart of the king is in the hand of the Lord; whithersoever He will He shall turn it*; and (Phil 2:13): *It is God Who worketh in you both to will and to accomplish.* Therefore man has not free-will. . . .

On the contrary, It is written (Sir 15:14): *God made man from the beginning, and left him in the hand of his own counsel;* and the gloss adds: *That is of his free-will.*

I answer that, Man has free-will: otherwise counsels, exhortations, commands, prohibitions, rewards and punishments would be in vain.[6] In order to make this evident,

---

[6] Note how basic, practical, and commonsensical St. Thomas' first argument is. Note also how he connects free will with reason. There is a popular misconception that sees reason as unfree and deterministic,

we must observe that some things act without judgment; as a stone moves downwards; and in like manner all things which lack knowledge. And some act from judgment, but not a free judgment; as brute animals. For the sheep, seeing the wolf, judges it a thing to be shunned, from a natural and not a free judgment, because it judges, not from reason, but from natural instinct. And the same thing is to be said of any judgment of brute animals. But man acts from judgment, because by his apprehensive power he judges that something should be avoided or sought. But because this judgment, in the case of some particular act, is not from a natural instinct, but from some act of comparison in the reason, therefore he acts from free judgment and retains the power of being inclined to various things. For reason in contingent matters may follow opposite courses, as we see in dialectic syllogisms and rhetorical [probable] arguments. Now particular operations are contingent, and therefore in such matters the judgment of reason may follow opposite courses, and is not determinate to one. And forasmuch as man is rational is it necessary that man have a free-will.

Reply Obj. 1. As we have said above (Q. 81, A. 3, *ad* 2), the sensitive appetite, though it obeys the reason, yet in a given case can resist by desiring what the reason forbids. This is therefore the good which man does not [do] when he wishes—namely, *not to desire against reason*, as Augustine says (*ibid.*).

Reply Obj. 2. Those words of the Apostle are not to be taken as though man does not wish or does not run of his free-will, but because the free-will is not sufficient thereto unless it be moved and helped by God.

Reply Obj. 3. Free-will is the cause of its own movement, because by his free-will man moves himself to act. But it does

---

and freedom as irrational and arbitrary. It arises from the nineteenth-century Romantic reaction against eighteenth-century classical rationalism and determinism.

not of necessity belong to liberty that what is free should be the first cause of itself, as neither for one thing to be cause of another need it be the first cause. God, therefore, is the first cause, Who moves causes both natural and voluntary. And just as by moving natural causes He does not prevent their acts being natural, so by moving voluntary causes He does not deprive their actions of being voluntary: but rather is He the cause of this very thing in them; for He operates in each thing according to its own nature.[7]. . .

---

[7] Note how simply and elegantly St. Thomas solves the thorny problem of reconciling human free will with divine causality. If God's being the first cause of the nature of dogs makes dogs doggy and not un-doggy, then God's being the first cause of human freedom makes freedom free, not un-free. Grace establishes nature rather than removing it.

How the Soul While
United to the Body Understands
Corporeal Things beneath It

FIRST ARTICLE

Whether the Soul Knows Bodies through the Intellect?

Objection 3. Further, the intellect is concerned with things that are necessary and unchangeable. But all bodies are mobile and changeable. Therefore the soul cannot know bodies through the intellect.[8]

On the contrary, Science is in the intellect. If, therefore, the intellect does not know bodies, it follows that there is no science of bodies; and thus perishes natural science, which treats of mobile bodies.

I answer that, It should be said in order to elucidate this question, that the early philosophers, who inquired into the natures of things, thought there was nothing in the world save bodies. And because they observed that all bodies are mobile, and considered them to be ever in a state of flux,

---

[8] This is Plato's position. Plato sharply separated knowledge of bodies, which was only sensory and probable, from knowledge of Forms, which was intellectual and certain; for he thought there could be no unchanging and certain knowledge of changing things.

St. Thomas possessed none of the writings of the pre-Socratics except the few quoted fragments in Aristotle, and none of Plato except the *Timaeus.* The works of Aristotle had been only recently and incompletely rediscovered. It is a testimony to the community and integrity of philosophers and historians of philosophy during the sixteen hundred years between the Greeks and St. Thomas that he had such an accurate understanding of their major teachings.

they were of opinion that we can have no certain knowledge of the true nature of things. For what is in a continual state of flux, cannot be grasped with any degree of certitude, for it passes away ere the mind can form a judgment thereon: according to the saying of Heraclitus, that *it is not possible twice to touch a drop of water in a passing torrent*, as the Philosopher relates (*Metaph.* iv, Did. iii. 5).

After these came Plato, who, wishing to save the certitude of our knowledge of truth through the intellect, maintained that, besides these things corporeal, there is another genus of beings, separate from matter and movement, which beings he called *species* or *ideas*, by participation of which each one of these singular and sensible things is said to be either a man, or a horse, or the like. Wherefore he said that sciences and definitions, and whatever appertains to the act of the intellect, are not referred to these sensible bodies, but to those beings immaterial and separate: so that according to this the soul does not understand these corporeal things, but the separate species thereof.[9]

Now this may be shown to be false for two reasons. First, because since those species are immaterial and immovable, knowledge of movement and matter would be excluded from science (which knowledge is proper to natural science), and likewise all demonstration through moving and material causes. Secondly, because it seems ridiculous, when we seek for knowledge of things which are to us manifest, to introduce other beings, which cannot be the substance

---

[9] This is why only mathematics and philosophy, but not the physical sciences, were taught in Plato's Academy, but physical sciences flourished in Aristotle's Lyceum.

N.b.: in listing two Aristotelian objections to Plato's theory of separate Forms in the next paragraph, St. Thomas is especially concerned to preserve scientific knowledge of nature. The problem is, how can we have truly scientific knowledge—i.e., universal, necessary, and unchanging knowledge—about particular, contingent, and changing things? See Objection 3.

of those others, since they differ from them essentially: so that granted that we have a knowledge of those separate substances, we cannot for that reason claim to form a judgment concerning these sensible things.

Now it seems that Plato strayed from the truth because, having observed that all knowledge takes place through some kind of similitude, he thought that the form of the thing known must of necessity be in the knower in the same manner as in the thing known.[10] Then he observed that the form of the thing understood is in the intellect under conditions of universality, immateriality, and immobility: which is apparent from the very operation of the intellect, whose act of understanding has a universal extension, and is subject to a certain amount of necessity: for the mode of action corresponds to the mode of the agent's form. Wherefore he concluded that the things which we understand must have in themselves an existence under the same conditions of immateriality and immobility.

But there is no necessity for this. For even in sensible things it is to be observed that the form is otherwise in one sensible than in another: for instance, whiteness may be of great intensity in one, and of a less intensity in another: in one we find whiteness with sweetness, in another without sweetness. In the same way the sensible form is conditioned differently in the thing which is external to the soul, and in the senses which receive the forms of sensible things without receiving matter, such as the color of gold without receiving gold.[11] So also the intellect, according to its own mode, receives under conditions of immateriality and immobility, the species of material and mobile bodies:

---

[10] Plato's implicit major premise. Philosophical refutation consists largely in making explicit your opponent's implicit assumptions and then criticizing them.

[11] I.e., even the senses perform some abstraction; so, a fortiori, does the intellect.

for the received is in the receiver according to the mode of the receiver. We must conclude, therefore, that through the intellect the soul knows bodies by a knowledge which is immaterial, universal, and necessary. . . .

Reply Obj. 3. Every movement presupposes something immovable:[12] for when a change of quality occurs, the substance remains unmoved; and when there is a change of substantial form, matter remains unmoved. Moreover the various conditions of mutable things are themselves immovable; for instance, though Socrates be not always sitting, yet it is an immovable truth that whenever he does sit he remains in one place. For this reason there is nothing to hinder our having an immovable science of movable things.

SIXTH ARTICLE

Whether Intellectual Knowledge Is Derived from Sensible Things?[13]

Objection 2. Further, Augustine says (*Gen. ad lit.* xii. 16): *We must not think that the body can make any impression on the spirit, as though the spirit were to supply the place of matter in regard to the body's action; for that which acts is in every way more excellent than that which it acts on.* Whence he concludes that

---

[12] That is, as an unchanging substratum. Otherwise it could not be truly said that *x* changes, for *x* would be in no sense still *x* after the change. This was Aristotle's solution to the puzzle of motion that bedeviled his predecessors—how can *x* become *y* while remaining *x*?—producing three inadequate pre-Aristotelian solutions: (1) Parmenides: motion is an illusion: (2) Heraclitus: *everything* moves (*panta rhei*); (3) Plato: there are two *separate* realms of reality: unmoving Forms and wholly moving natural substances. Note how each solution was closer to the truth than its predecessors.

[13] Again note St. Thomas' balance: Article 5 (the Platonic-Augustinian point) must be supplemented by Article 6 (the Aristotelian point) and vice versa.

the body does not cause its image in the spirit, but the spirit causes it in itself. Therefore intellectual knowledge is not derived from sensible things.

Objection 3. Further, an effect does not surpass the power of its cause. But intellectual knowledge extends beyond sensible things: for we understand some things which cannot be perceived by the senses. Therefore intellectual knowledge is not derived from sensible things.

On the contrary, The Philosopher says (*Metaph.* i. 1; *Poster.* ii. 15) that the principle of knowledge is in the senses.

I answer that, On this point the philosophers held three opinions. For Democritus held that *all knowledge is caused by* [material] *images issuing from the bodies we think of and entering into our souls,* as Augustine says in his letter to Dioscorus (cxviii. 4). And Aristotle says (*De Somn. et Vigil.*) that Democritus held that knowledge is caused by a *discharge of images.* And the reason for this opinion was that both Democritus and the other early philosophers did not distinguish between intellect and sense, as Aristotle relates (*De Anima* iii. 3). Consequently, since the sense is affected by the sensible, they thought that all our knowledge is affected by this mere impression brought about by sensible things. Which impression Democritus held to be caused by a discharge of images.

Plato, on the other hand, held that the intellect is distinct from the senses: and that it is an immaterial power not making use of a corporeal organ for its action. And since the incorporeal cannot be affected by the corporeal,[14] he held that intellectual knowledge is not brought about by sensible things affecting the intellect, but by separate intelligible forms being participated by the intellect, as we have said above (AA. 4, 5). Moreover he held that sense is a power operating of itself. Consequently neither is sense, since it is

---

[14] Plato was right in these three preceding points, but wrong in thinking they necessitated the conclusion that follows the footnote.

a spiritual power, affected by the sensible: but the sensible organs are affected by the sensible, the result being that the soul is in a way roused to form within itself the species of the sensible. Augustine seems to touch on this opinion (*Gen. ad lit.* xii. 24) where he says that the *body feels not, but the soul through the body, which it makes use of as a kind of messenger, for reproducing within itself what is announced from without.* Thus according to Plato, neither does intellectual knowledge proceed from sensible knowledge, nor sensible knowledge exclusively from sensible things; but these rouse the sensible soul to the sentient act, while the senses rouse the intellect to the act of understanding.

Aristotle chose a middle course.[15] For with Plato he agreed that intellect and sense are different. But he held that the sense has not its proper operation without the co-operation of the body; so that to feel is not an act of the soul alone, but of the *composite*. And he held the same in regard to all the operations of the sensitive part. Since, therefore, it is not unreasonable that the sensible objects which are outside the soul should produce some effect in the *composite*, Aristotle agreed with Democritus in this, that the operations of the sensitive part are caused by the impression of the sensible on the sense: not by a discharge, as Democritus said, but by some kind of operation. For Democritus maintained that every operation is by way of a discharge of atoms, as we gather from *De Gener.* i. 8. But Aristotle held that the intellect has an operation which is independent of the body's co-operation. Now nothing corporeal can make an impression on the incorporeal. And therefore in order to cause the intellectual operation, according to Aristotle, the impression caused by the sensible does not suffice, but something more noble is required, for *the agent is more noble than the patient*, as he says (*ibid.* 5). Not, indeed, in the sense

---

[15] As usual. This sentence sums up Aristotle's position vis-à-vis most other philosophers both before him and after him.

that the intellectual operation is effected in us by the mere impression of some superior beings, as Plato held; but that the higher and more noble agent which he calls the active intellect, of which we have spoken above (Q. 79, AA. 3, 4), causes the phantasms received from the senses to be actually intelligible, by a process of abstraction.

According to this opinion, then, on the part of the phantasms, intellectual knowledge is caused by the senses. But since the phantasms cannot of themselves affect the passive intellect, and require to be made actually intelligible by the active intellect, it cannot be said that sensible knowledge is the total and perfect cause of intellectual knowledge, but rather that it is in a way the material cause. . . .

Reply Obj. 2. In this passage Augustine speaks not of intellectual but of imaginary knowledge.[16] . . .

Reply Obj. 3. Sensitive knowledge is not the entire cause of intellectual knowledge. And therefore it is not strange that intellectual knowledge should extend further than sensitive knowledge.

---

[16] A charitable but questionable interpretation of Augustine.

Of the Mode and Order
of Understanding

FIRST ARTICLE

*Whether Our Intellect Understands Corporeal and
Material Things by Abstraction from Phantasms?*

Objection 1. It would seem that our intellect does not understand corporeal and material things by abstraction from
the phantasms. For the intellect is false if it understands an
object otherwise than as it really is. Now the forms of material things do not exist as abstracted from the particular
things represented by the phantasms. Therefore, if we understand material things by abstraction of the species from
the phantasm, there will be error in the intellect.

Objection 2. Further, material things are those natural
things which include matter in their definition. But nothing can be understood apart from that which enters into its
definition. Therefore material things cannot be understood
apart from matter. Now matter is the principle of individ-
ualization. Therefore material things cannot be understood
by abstraction of the universal from the particular, which
is the process whereby the intelligible species is abstracted
from the phantasm.[17]. . .

On the contrary, The Philosopher says (*De Anima* iii. 4)
that *things are intelligible in proportion as they are separable from
matter.* Therefore material things must needs be understood
according as they are abstracted from matter and from material images, namely, phantasms.

---

[17] Both these two Objections assume a simple "copy" theory of
knowledge.

I answer that, As stated above (Q. 84, A. 7), the object of knowledge is proportionate to the power of knowledge. Now there are three grades of the cognitive powers. For one cognitive power, namely, the sense, is the act of a corporeal organ. And therefore the object of every sensitive power is a form as existing in corporeal matter. And since such matter is the principle of individuality, therefore every power of the sensitive part can only have knowledge of the individual.[18] There is another grade of cognitive power which is neither the act of a corporeal organ, nor in any way connected with corporeal matter; such is the angelic intellect, the object of whose cognitive power is therefore a form existing apart from matter: for though angels know material things, yet they do not know them save in something immaterial, namely, either in themselves or in God.[19] But the human intellect holds a middle place:[20] for it is not the act of an organ,[21] yet it is a power of the soul which is the form of the body,[22] as is clear from what we have said above (Q. 76, A. 1). And therefore it is proper to it to know a form existing individually in corporeal matter, but not as existing in this individual matter.[23] But to know what is in individual matter, not as existing in such matter, is to abstract the form from individual matter which is represented by the phantasms. Therefore we must needs say that our intellect understands material things by abstracting from the phantasms; and through material things thus considered we acquire some knowledge of immaterial things, just as,

---

[18] I.e., we cannot *see* treeness, only trees.

[19] Angels know everything they know, even facts about the material world, by a kind of mental telepathy.

[20] A key principle; again the cosmic hierarchy gives perspective to St. Thomas' Aristotelian "golden mean". (Cf. n. 15.)

[21] (As the senses are).

[22] (Unlike the intellect of an angel).

[23] I.e., not limited to this particular instance.

on the contrary, angels know material things through the immaterial.

But Plato, considering only the immateriality of the human intellect, and not its being in a way united to the body, held that the objects of the intellect are separate ideas; and that we understand not by abstraction, but by participating things abstract, as stated above (Q. 84, A. 1).

Reply Obj. 1. Abstraction may occur in two ways: First, by way of composition and division;[24] thus we may understand that one thing does not exist in some other, or that it is separate therefrom. Secondly, by way of simple and absolute consideration;[25] thus understand one thing without considering the other. Thus for the intellect to abstract one from another things which are not really abstract from one another, does, in the first mode of abstraction, imply falsehood. But, in the second mode of abstraction, for the intellect to abstract things which are not really abstract from one another, does not involve falsehood, as clearly appears in the case of the senses. For if we understood or said that color is not in a colored body, or that it is separate from it, there would be error in this opinion or assertion. But if we consider color and its properties, without reference to the apple which is colored; or if we express in word what we thus understand, there is no error in such an opinion or assertion, because an apple is not essential to color, and therefore color can be understood independently of the apple. Likewise, the things which belong to the species of a material thing, such as a stone, or a man, or a horse, can be thought of apart from the individualizing principles which do not belong to the notion of the species. This is what we

---

[24] This "first way" is a negative *judgment*, the "second act of the mind".

[25] The "second way" is a *concept* abstracted from its individual concrete instances—something within the realm of "the first act of the mind": conception, apprehension, understanding.

mean by abstracting the universal from the particular, or the intelligible species from phantasm; that is, by considering the nature of the species apart from its individual qualities represented by the phantasms. If, therefore, the intellect is said to be false when it understands a thing otherwise than as it is, that is so, if the word *otherwise* refers to the thing understood; for the intellect is false when it understands a thing otherwise than as it is; and so the intellect would be false if it abstracted the species of a stone from its matter in such a way as to regard the species as not existing in matter, as Plato held. But it is not so, if the word *otherwise* be taken as referring to the one who understands. For it is quite true that the mode of understanding, in one who understands, is not the same as the mode of a thing in existing: since the thing understood is immaterially in the one who understands, according to the mode of the intellect, and not materially, according to the mode of a material thing.

Reply Obj. 2. Some have thought that the species of a natural thing is a form only, and that matter is not part of the species [essence]. If that were so, matter would not enter into the definition of natural things. Therefore it must be said otherwise, that matter is twofold, common, and *signate* or individual; common, such as flesh and bone; and individual, as this flesh and these bones. The intellect therefore abstracts the species of a natural thing from the individual sensible matter, but not from the common sensible matter; for example, it abstracts the species of man from *this flesh and these bones*, which do not belong to the species as such, but to the individual (*Metaph.* vii, *Did.* vi. 10), and need not be considered in the species: whereas the species of man cannot be abstracted by the intellect from *flesh and bones*.

Mathematical species, however, can be abstracted by the intellect from sensible matter, not only from individual, but also from common matter; not from common intelligible matter, but only from individual matter. For sensible matter is corporeal matter as subject to sensible qualities, such as being cold or hot, hard or soft, and the like: while intelligible matter is substance as subject to quantity. Now it is manifest that quantity is in substance before other sensible qualities are. Hence quantities, such as number, dimension, and figures, which are the terminations of quantity, can be considered apart from sensible qualities; and this is to abstract them from sensible matter; but they cannot be considered without understanding the substance which is subject to the quantity; for that would be to abstract them from common intelligible matter. Yet they can be considered apart from this or that substance; for that is to abstract them from individual intelligible matter. But some things can be abstracted even from common intelligible matter, such as *being, unity, power, act*, and the like; all these exist without matter, as is plain regarding immaterial things.[26] Because Plato failed to consider the twofold kind of abstraction, as above explained (*ad* 1), he held that all those things which we have stated to be abstracted by the intellect, are abstract in reality. . . .

---

[26] St. Thomas distinguishes (a) individual sensible matter: this flesh and these bones; (b) common sensible matter: flesh and bones in general; (c) common intelligible matter: quantified substance.

The senses do not abstract from (a) or (b) or (c).

The physical sciences abstract from (a) but not from (b) or (c).

The mathematical sciences abstract from (a) and (b) but not from (c).

Metaphysics abstracts from (a) and (b) and (c).

Physics, mathematics, and metaphysics represent the three degrees of abstraction.

SECOND ARTICLE

Whether the Intelligible Species Abstracted from the Phantasm Is Related to Our Intellect As That Which Is Understood?[27]

Objection 2. Further, what is actually understood must be in something; else it would be nothing. But it is not in something outside the soul: for, since what is outside the soul is material, nothing therein can be actually understood. Therefore what is actually understood is in the intellect. Consequently it can be nothing else than the aforesaid intelligible species. . . .

On the contrary, The intelligible species is to the intellect what the sensible image is to the sense. But the sensible image is not what is perceived, but rather that by which sense perceives. Therefore the intelligible species is not what is

---

[27] This is perhaps the most important article in St. Thomas' epistemology, historically speaking, for it is his alternative to most classical modern epistemology, which in turn is most of classical modern philosophy. Modern epistemology is haunted by the spectre of skepticism and even solipsism because of its constant subjectivistic tendency. This, in turn, stems above all from the "thingification of ideas", the tendency to treat ideas not as intentional *signs* (pure signs, mere signs, "formal signs" in technical Thomistic terminology), but as *things* intended (known) before they intend other things (technically, as "material signs"); not as means (*quo*) of knowing objects, but as objects (*quod*) known. Indeed, this is the very first thesis of Locke's theory of knowledge: "Idea = object of knowledge". St. Thomas takes an alternative path right here at the beginning, defining an idea (or "intelligible species") not as "that which" (*id quod*) is understood, i.e., as an object, but as "that by which" (*id quo*) some objectively real thing is understood. If all we knew primarily and directly were our own ideas, skepticism would be inevitable, eventually, for we would be like prisoners in jail cells, seeing only pictures of the outside world on TV screens and never able to get out of jail and see the real world directly to know whether the TV images are true or false.

actually understood, but that by which the intellect understands.[28]

I answer that, Some have asserted that our intellectual faculties know only the impression made on them; as, for example, that sense is cognizant only of the impression made on its own organ. According to this theory, the intellect understands only its own impression, namely, the intelligible species which it has received, so that this species is what is understood.[29]

This is, however, manifestly false for two reasons. First, because the things we understand are the objects of science; therefore if what we understand is merely the intelligible species in the soul, it would follow that every science would not be concerned with objects outside the soul, but only with the intelligible species within the soul. . . . Secondly, it is untrue, because it would lead to the opinion of the ancients [the Sophists] who maintained that *whatever seems, is true* [cf. Arist., *Metaph.* iii. 5], and that consequently contradictories are true simultaneously. For if the faculty knows its own impression only, it can judge of that only. Now a thing seems, according to the impression made on the cognitive faculty. Consequently the cognitive faculty will always

---

[28] The analogy between sense images and ideas ("intelligible species") is not perfect. We cannot by reflection sense the means of our sensing, viz., sense images (see the last half of the last paragraph of the "*I answer that*"); but *ideas,* though not primary objects known, *can* be secondary objects known, reflectively, after some real primary object is known. Sense images, on the other hand, are never sensed even as secondary objects; for the sense image itself has no size, shape, or weight as sensible objects have.

[29] The "intelligible species" is the form, abstracted by the mind from the real substance existing in nature. Thus, according to this semi-subjectivistic, semi-skeptical epistemology St. Thomas is criticizing, we cannot know real things as they really are (what Kant calls "things-in-themselves"). St. Thomas argues that this position would lead to two absurd conclusions (in the next paragraph).

judge of its own impression as such; and so every judgment will be true: for instance, if taste perceived only its own impression, when anyone with a healthy taste perceives that honey is sweet, he would judge truly; and if anyone with a corrupt taste perceives that honey is bitter, this would be equally true; for each would judge according to the impression on his taste. Thus every opinion would be equally true; in fact, every sort of apprehension.[30]

Therefore it must be said that the intelligible species is related to the intellect as that by which it understands.[31]. . . But since the intellect reflects upon itself, by such reflection it understands both its own act of intelligence, and the species by which it understands. Thus the intelligible species is that which is understood secondarily; but that which is primarily understood is the object, of which the species is the likeness. . . .

Reply Obj. 2. In these words *the thing actually understood* there is a double implication: the thing which is understood, and the fact that it is understood. In like manner the words *abstract universal* imply two things, the nature of a thing and its abstraction or universality. Therefore the nature itself to which it occurs to be understood, abstracted or considered as universal is only in individuals; but that it is understood, abstracted or considered as universal is in the intellect. We

---

[30] In other words, "true" means only "true to me". Thus no one is ever *wrong*, for there is no knowledge of objective reality to judge a subjective opinion as failing to conform to it. This is a very popular philosophy among American students: see the first sentence of Alan Bloom's bestseller, *The Closing of the American Mind*. St. Thomas' argument against this relativism is simple and logical: it violates the law of non-contradiction. Another simple argument to the same effect is that if every opinion is equally true, then this opinion is also true: that some opinions are false.

[31] St. Thomas thus implicitly sees ideas as dynamic rather than static, as acts (or instruments) of knowing rather than objects known (except by a second, reflexive act):

see something similar to this in the senses. For the sight sees the color of the apple apart from its smell. If therefore it be asked where is the color which is seen apart from the smell, it is quite clear that the color which is seen is only in the apple: but that it be perceived apart from the smell, this is owing to the sight, forasmuch as the faculty of sight receives the likeness of color and not of smell. In like manner humanity understood is only in this or that man; but that humanity be apprehended without conditions of individuality, that is, that it be abstracted and consequently considered as universal, occurs to humanity inasmuch as it is brought under the consideration of the intellect.[32]. . .

ST. THOMAS:

OPPONENTS:

[32] "Appleness" exists only in individual apples. But the intellect can abstract, or focus on the form alone *without the matter*; thus the form *as known* is universal (for *matter* is what individuates form). Universality is in the mind, not in the world.

VII. ETHICS

❧

QUESTION 2

Of Those Things in Which Man's Happiness Consists[1]

FIRST ARTICLE

Whether Man's Happiness Consists in Wealth?

Objection 1. It would seem that man's happiness consists in wealth. For since happiness is man's last end, it must consist in that which has the greatest hold on man's affections. Now this is wealth: for it is written (Qo 10:19): *All things obey money.*[2] Therefore man's happiness consists in wealth.

---

[1] This Question (2) is the most masterfully condensed summary of the basic answers which philosophers in their writings and people in their lives have always given to the most important question in life, the question of the *summum bonum*, the greatest good, final end, meaning and purpose of life. I have included an unusually large number of footnotes on this Question not because it is obscure but because it is crucially important. Moses, Solomon, Buddha, Krishna, Confucius, Lao-tzu, St. Paul, St. Augustine, Mohammed, Machiavelli, Hobbes, Bacon, Pascal, Kierkegaard, Nietzsche, Sartre, Marx—all sages and pseudosages answer this question, and their answer colors and determines the rest of their practical philosophy.

[2] The ancient version of "Everything has a price tag", or even "Every man has his price." N.b.: the arguments of all three objections are only clues; they find some feature common to the *summum bonum* and wealth. As demonstrations, they commit the fallacy of undistributed

Objection 2. Further, according to Boëthius (*De Consol.* iii), happiness is *a state of life made perfect by the aggregate of all good things.* Now money seems to be the means of possessing all things: for, as the Philosopher says (*Ethic.* v. 5), money was invented, that it might be a sort of guarantee for the acquisition of whatever man desires.[3] Therefore happiness consists in wealth.

Objection 3. Further, since the desire for the sovereign good never fails, it seems to be infinite. But this is the case with riches more than anything else; since *a covetous man shall not be satisfied with riches* (Qo 5:9). Therefore happiness consists in wealth.

On the contrary, Man's good consists in retaining happiness rather than in spreading it. But as Boëthius says (*De Consol.* ii), *wealth shines in giving rather than in hoarding: for the miser is hateful, whereas the generous man is applauded.* Therefore man's happiness does not consist in wealth.[4]

I answer that, It is impossible for man's happiness to con-

---

middle: the *summum bonum* is *x*, wealth is *x*, therefore wealth is the *summum bonum*. The same is true for most of the Objections in subsequent Articles in this Question.

[3] I.e., money is like an umbrella, over everything. Money can buy anything money can buy. Since it is its universality that seems to qualify it as the *summum bonum*, St. Thomas' reply is that its very universality is deceptive. It can buy *only* "anything money can buy" (Reply 2); the umbrella is really too small.

[4] Money, unlike happiness, is good only when spent, not kept. N.b.: the arguments in the "*On the contrary*" sections are not *demonstrations* from cause to effect, but often from effect to cause. The real cause or reason why wealth is not the *summum bonum* is given in the "*I answer that*". The "*On the contrary*" only points to a clue to the fact that wealth is not happiness, but not the real reason or cause.

When St. Thomas says that happiness, unlike wealth, is good when possessed, not when spread, he does not mean that our happiness is not in fact increased when we make others happy, but that the essential meaning of "happiness" is the satisfaction of an individual's desires. These may and should include the desire to make others happy too.

sist in wealth. For wealth is twofold, as the Philosopher says
(*Polit.* i. 3), viz., natural and artificial. Natural wealth is that
which serves man as a remedy for his natural wants: such
as food, drink, clothing, dwellings, and such like, while artificial wealth is that which is not a direct help to nature,
as money, but is invented by the art of man, for the conve-
nience of exchange, and as a measure of things salable.[5]

Now it is evident that man's happiness cannot consist in
natural wealth. For wealth of this kind is sought for the sake
of something else, viz., as a support of human nature: consequently it cannot be man's last end, rather is it ordained
to man as to its end. Wherefore in the order of nature, all
such things are below man, and made for him, according to
Psalm 8:8: *Thou hast subjected all things under his feet.*[6]

And as to artificial wealth, it is not sought save for the
sake of natural wealth; since man would not seek it except because, by its means, he procures for himself the nec-
essaries of life. Consequently much less can it be considered in the light of the last end.[7] Therefore it is impossible

---

[5] The simple and obvious distinction between natural wealth and
artificial wealth (and between natural and artificial anything, such as
sex, death, and birth control) is largely forgotten, in practice, in a cap-
italistic and industrial society. In a society like ours, which gives such
prominence to artificial wealth, greed is a very great spiritual danger.
For the desire for artificial wealth is unlimited, but the desire for natural wealth, however greedy, is always limited (Reply 3). There is never
enough money, but there is often enough food. The good society would
foster neither riches (of excess artificial wealth) nor poverty (of needed
natural wealth).

[6] Man is an end, things (wealth) are means. For man to serve things
is to reverse the order of reality. St. Thomas here assumes that man is
an end, not a means. Yet he is not the final end. In Article 7, "*On the
contrary*", he says that man is to be loved not for his own sake (as final
end) but for God's sake. God is to be adored, man loved, and things
used. Two of the commonest and deadliest errors are to adore man, or
to use man and love things.

[7] This is a good example of the *a minore* argument: if natural wealth

for happiness, which is the last end of man, to consist in wealth.

Reply Obj. 1. All material things obey money, so far as the multitude of fools is concerned, who know no other than material goods, which can be obtained for money. But we should take our estimation of human goods not from the foolish but from the wise: just as it is for a person, whose sense of taste is in good order, to judge whether a thing is palatable.[8]

Reply Obj. 2. All things salable can be had for money: not so spiritual things, which cannot be sold. Hence it is written (Prov 17:16): *What doth it avail a fool to have riches, seeing he cannot buy wisdom.*

Reply Obj. 3. The desire for natural riches is not infinite: because they suffice for nature in a certain measure. But the desire for artificial wealth is infinite, for it is the servant of disordered concupiscence, which is not curbed, as the Philosopher makes clear (*Polit.* i. 3). Yet this desire for wealth is infinite otherwise than the desire for the sovereign good. For the more perfectly the sovereign good is possessed, the more it is loved, and other things despised: because the more we possess it, the more we know it. Hence it is written, (Sir 24:29): *They that eat me shall yet hunger.* Whereas in the desire for wealth and for whatsoever temporal goods,

---

is not the *summum bonum* because it is a mere means, not an end, then how much less can artificial wealth be the *summum bonum*, since it is a mere means to this means (natural wealth).

N.b.: St. Thomas takes the candidates for the *summum bonum* in a deliberate order: from the most foolish and external to the least foolish and most internal. Wealth is the farthest of all from happiness, yet it is the most popular candidate for that exalted office (see Objection 1 and Reply). Pleasure is much closer, since it is at least a *property* of happiness, flowing from it (Article 6, "*I answer that*")—though this is not just bodily pleasure.

[8] St. Thomas' answer to the popular skeptical question, "Who's to say?"

the contrary is the case: for when we already possess them, we despise them, and seek others:[9] which is the sense of Our Lord's words (Jn 4:13): *Whosoever drinketh of this water*, by which temporal goods are signified, *shall thirst again*. The reason of this is that we realize more their insufficiency when we possess them: and this very fact shows that they are imperfect, and that the sovereign good does not consist therein.[10]

SECOND ARTICLE

Whether Man's Happiness Consists in Honors?[11]

Objection 1. It would seem that man's happiness consists in honors. For happiness or bliss is *the reward of virtue*, as the Philosopher says (*Ethic.* i. 9). But honor more than anything else seems to be that by which virtue is rewarded, as the Philosopher says (*Ethic.* iv. 3). Therefore happiness consists especially in honor.

Objection 2. Further, that which belongs to God and to persons of great excellence seems especially to be happiness, which is the perfect good. But that is honor, as the Philoso-

---

[9] N.b.: the same is true of "sex objects" as of money: they are far less desirable once "attained" than when unattained and desired. The true good is just the opposite. St. Thomas would probably say that our society treats sex like money (as a medium of exchange) and money like sex (for under capitalism, money can reproduce itself in interest [usury], which St. Thomas, like most pre-modern Christian, Jewish, and Muslim thinkers, considered unnatural).

[10] Thus experience is an honest teacher, especially the experience of failure and unhappiness, as Augustine found in his life (cf. *Confessions*) and many find today.

[11] The ancient version of honor ("high marks" from others) is hierarchical—being honored for being *superior*—while the more usual modern version is egalitarian—being accepted as "one of the crowd". But both versions remain subject to the same arguments here.

pher says (*Ethic.* iv. 3). Moreover, the Apostle says (1 Tim 1:17): *To . . . the only God be honor and glory.* Therefore happiness consists in honor.

Objection 3. Further, that which man desires above all is happiness. But nothing seems more desirable to man than honor: since man suffers loss in all other things, lest he should suffer loss of honor.[12] Therefore happiness consists in honor.

On the contrary, Happiness is in the happy. But honor is not in the honored, but rather in him who honors,[13] and who offers deference to the person honored, as the Philosopher says (*Ethic.* i. 5). Therefore happiness does not consist in honor.

I answer that, It is impossible for happiness to consist in honor. For honor is given to a man on account of some excellence in him; and consequently it is a sign and attestation of the excellence that is in the person honored.[14] Now a man's excellence is in proportion, especially, to his happiness, which is man's perfect good; and to its parts, *i.e.*, those goods by which he has a certain share of happiness. And therefore honor can result from happiness, but happiness cannot principally consist therein.

Reply Obj. 1. As the Philosopher says (*ibid.*), honor is not that reward of virtue, for which the virtuous work: but they receive honor from men by way of reward, *as from those who have nothing greater to offer.* But virtue's true reward is happiness itself, for which the virtuous work: whereas if they

---

[12] This Objection, like Objection 1 in Article 1, confuses the *desired* with the *desirable*, or wants with needs.

[13] I.e., honor is external and happiness is internal.

[14] Working for a grade in a course rather than for wisdom is an example of wrongly reversing the sign and the thing signified. Going on a vacation just to take pictures of it is another. Being good just so that people will honor you, or to "get along with people", is a third, very popular form of the same mistake.

worked for honor, it would no longer be a virtue, but [the vice of] ambition.

Reply Obj. 2. Honor is due to God and to persons of great excellence as a sign of attestation of excellence already existing: not that honor makes them excellent.

Reply Obj. 3. That man desires honor above all else, arises from his natural desire for happiness, from which honor results, as stated above. Wherefore man seeks to be honored especially by the wise, on whose judgment he believes himself to be excellent or happy.[15]

THIRD ARTICLE

Whether Man's Happiness Consists in Fame or Glory?[16]

Objection 1. It would seem that man's happiness consists in glory. For happiness seems to consist in that which is paid to the saints for the trials they have undergone in the world. But this is glory: for the Apostle says (Rom 8:18) *The sufferings of this time are not worthy to be compared with the glory to come, that shall be revealed in us*. Therefore happiness consists in glory.

Objection 2. Further, good is diffusive of itself, as stated by Dionysius (*Div. Nom.* iv.). But man's good is spread abroad in the knowledge of others by glory more than by anything

---

[15] Even in terms of how men *do* behave, much less how they *should* behave, they show that they do not pursue honor as the *summum bonum*, since if they did, it would not matter who gave them the honor. The fact that they want to be honored by the wise, who know the truth, rather than fools, means they want to be honored for being truly happy (i.e., objectively good, blessed, worthy of honor).

[16] Though "honor" and "fame" are similar, they are not identical. We can be honored (by a few) without being famous (to the wider world), or famous without being honored (if the fame is negative or neutral in value). "Fame" here, however, is positive: honor multiplied, quantity added to quality (see "*I answer that*", second sentence).

else: since, according to Ambrose [Augustine,—*Contra Maxim. Arian.* ii. 13], glory consists *in being well known and praised.* Therefore man's happiness consists in glory [cf. n. 11].

Objection 3. Further, happiness is the most enduring good. Now this seems to be fame or glory; because by this men attain to eternity after a fashion. Hence Boëthius says (*De Consol.* ii): *You seem to beget unto yourselves eternity, when you think of your fame in future time.* Therefore man's happiness consists in fame or glory.

On the contrary, Happiness is man's true good. But it happens that fame or glory is false:[17] for as Boëthius says (*De Consol.* iii), *many owe their renown to the lying reports spread among the people. Can anything be more shameful? For those who receive false fame, must needs blush at their own praise.* Therefore man's happiness does not consist in fame or glory.

$\longrightarrow$ *I answer that,* Man's happiness cannot consist in human fame or glory. For glory consists *in being well known and praised,* as Ambrose [Augustine,—*Contra Maxim. Arian.* ii. 13] says. Now the thing known is related to human knowledge otherwise than to God's knowledge: for human knowledge is caused by the things known, whereas God's knowledge is the cause of the things known.[18] Wherefore the perfection of human good, which is called happiness, cannot be caused by human knowledge: but rather human knowledge

---

[17] Note the use of "true" and "false" here not as characterizing *propositions* but *realities,* as authentic and inauthentic (cf. I, 16, "*I answer that*").

[18] God caused the universe by knowing it into existence, i.e., by uttering the mental word, according to Genesis. Things exist, and are *what* they are, because God knows them as such (e.g., dogs are doggy because God "thought them up"). Human knowledge is similar in creative art; but in science and in common sense, human knowledge is caused by and conforms to its object: we think "the sky is blue" because the sky *is* blue. This metaphysical principle entails the conclusion that fame cannot cause happiness, since fame is a form of human knowledge, and human knowledge does not cause its object but is caused by it.

of another's happiness proceeds from, and, in a fashion, is caused by, human happiness itself, inchoate or perfect. Consequently man's happiness cannot consist in fame or glory.

On the other hand, man's good depends on God's knowledge as its cause. And therefore man's beatitude depends, as on its cause, on the glory which man has with God;[19] according to Psalm 90:15, 16: *I will deliver him, and I will glorify him; I will fill him with length of days, and I will show him my salvation.*

Furthermore, we must observe that human knowledge often fails, especially in contingent singulars, such as are human acts. For this reason human glory is frequently deceptive. But since God cannot be deceived, His glory is always true; hence it is written (2 Cor 10:18): *He . . . is approved . . . whom God commendeth.*

Reply Obj. 1. The Apostle speaks, then, not of the glory which is with men, but of the glory which is from God, with His Angels. Hence it is written (Mk 8:38): *The Son of Man shall confess him in the glory of His Father, before His angels.*

Reply Obj. 2. A man's good which, through fame or glory, is in the knowledge of many, if this knowledge be true, must needs be derived from good existing in the man himself: and hence it presupposes perfect or inchoate happiness. But if the knowledge be false, it does not harmonize with the thing: and thus good does not exist in him who is looked upon as famous. Hence it follows that fame can nowise make man happy.

Reply Obj. 3. Fame has no stability; in fact, it is easily ruined by false report. And if sometimes it endures, this is by accident. But happiness endures of itself, and for ever.

---

[19] This praise and glory from God is an ingredient in supreme happiness (1) because God's knowledge causes reality rather than reflecting it, and (2) because each of the inadequate candidates for happiness is included, transformed, and perfected in true happiness as an ingredient.

FOURTH ARTICLE

Whether Man's Happiness Consists in Power?[20]

Objection 1. It would seem that happiness consists in power. For all things desire to become like to God, as to their last end and first beginning. But men who are in power seem, on account of the similarity of power, to be most like to God:[21] hence also in Scripture they are called *gods* (Ex 22:28),—*Thou shalt not speak ill of the gods.* Therefore happiness consists in power.

Objection 2. Further, happiness is the perfect good. But the highest perfection for man is to be able to rule others; which belongs to those who are in power. Therefore happiness consists in power.

Objection 3. Further, since happiness is supremely desirable, it is contrary to that which is before all to be shunned. But, more than aught else, men shun servitude, which is contrary to power. Therefore happiness consists in power.

On the contrary, Happiness is the perfect good. But power is most imperfect. For as Boëthius says (*De Consol.* iii), *the power of man cannot relieve the gnawings of care, nor can it avoid the thorny path of anxiety:* and further on: *Think you a man is powerful who is surrounded by attendants, whom he inspires with fear indeed, but whom he fears still more?*[22] Therefore happiness does not consist in power.

I answer that, It is impossible for happiness to consist in power; and this for two reasons. First because power has the nature of principle, as is stated in *Metaph.* v. 12, whereas hap-

---

[20] What modern thinkers usually mean by "freedom" comes under this heading (cf. especially Objection 3).

[21] N.b.: we spontaneously think of this attribute before any other, even goodness, for we call Him "*Almighty* God", but use "*Good* God" as a mere expletive!

[22] Cf. Hegel's famous "master-slave dialectic" (the master is really the enslaved) and the maxim "Uneasy lies the head that wears the crown."

piness has the nature of last end.—Secondly, because power has relation to [is open to either] good and evil: whereas happiness is man's proper and perfect good. Wherefore some happiness might consist in the good use of power, which is by virtue, rather than in power itself.

Now four general reasons may be given to prove that happiness consists in none of the foregoing external goods. First, because, since happiness is man's supreme good, it is incompatible with any evil.[23] Now all the foregoing can be found both in good and in evil men.—Secondly, because, since it is the nature of happiness to *satisfy of itself*, as stated in *Ethic*. i. 7, having gained happiness, man cannot lack any needful good. But after acquiring any one of the foregoing, man may still lack many goods that are necessary to him; for instance, wisdom, bodily health, and such like. —Thirdly, because, since happiness is the perfect good, no evil can accrue to anyone therefrom. This cannot be said of the foregoing: for it is written (Qo 5:12) that *riches* are sometimes *kept to the hurt of the owner*; and the same may be said of the other three.—Fourthly, because man is ordained to happiness through principles that are in him; since he is ordained thereto naturally. Now the four goods mentioned above are due rather to external causes, and in most cases to fortune [chance]; for which reason they are called goods of fortune.[24] Therefore it is evident that happiness nowise consists in the foregoing.

Reply Obj. 1. God's power is His goodness:[25] hence He cannot use His power otherwise than well. But it is not so with men. Consequently it is not enough for man's happi-

---

[23] Note the difference between (true, objective) *happiness* and mere (subjective) *contentment* here.

[24] Note how this shallow error is implicitly at the root of the English word "happiness", which derives from "hap" (chance or fortune).

[25] For all of God's attributes are one with each other, since they are all one with His essence (cf. I, 3, 7).

ness, that he become like God in power, unless he become like Him in goodness also.

Reply Obj. 2. Just as it is a very good thing for a man to make good use of power in ruling many, so is it a very bad thing if he makes a bad use of it.[26] And so it is that power is [open] towards good and evil.

Reply Obj. 3. Servitude is a hindrance to the good use of power: therefore is it that men naturally shun it; not because man's supreme good consists in power.

FIFTH ARTICLE

Whether Man's Happiness Consists in Any Bodily Good?[27]

Objection 1. It would seem that man's happiness consists in bodily goods. For it is written (Sir 30:16): *There is no riches above the riches of the health of the body.*[28] But happiness consists in that which is best. Therefore it consists in the health of the body. . . .

On the contrary, Man surpasses all other animals in regard to happiness. But in bodily goods he is surpassed by many animals; for instance, by the elephant in longevity, by the

---

[26] Cf. Lord Acton's maxim, "All power tends to corrupt, and absolute power corrupts absolutely." (Only God is incorruptible.)

[27] *Pleasure* is considered in Article 6, not the Article on "bodily goods" (5), because St. Thomas means by "bodily goods" what is objectively good for the body—essentially, health—rather than subjective feelings of enjoyment.

[28] To quote still another maxim, "If you have your health, you have everything." The plethora of maxims relevant to this Question shows that it is a question most men have thought about; in fact, it is probably the most popular of all the questions philosophers ask, since it is the most practical for everyone.

lion in strength, by the stag in fleetness.[29] Therefore man's
happiness does not consist in goods of the body.

I answer that, It is impossible for man's happiness to consist in the goods of the body; and this for two reasons. First,
because, if a thing be ordained to another as to its end, its last
end cannot consist in the [mere] preservation of its being.
Hence a captain does not intend as a last end, the preservation of the ship entrusted to him, since a ship is ordained
to something else as its end, viz., to navigation.[30] Now just
as the ship is entrusted to the captain that he may steer its
course, so man is given over to his will and reason; according to Sirach 15:14; *God made man from the beginning and left
him in the hand of his own counsel.* Now it is evident that man
is ordained to something as his end: since man is not the
supreme good.[31] Therefore the last end of man's reason and
will cannot be the preservation of man's being.

Secondly, because, granted that the end of man's will and
reason be the preservation of man's being, it could not be
said that the end of man is some good of the body. For man's
being consists in soul and body; and though the being of
the body depends on the soul, yet the being of the human
soul depends not on the body, as shown above (I, Q. 75,
A. 2); and the very body is for the soul, as matter for its
form, and the instruments for the man that puts them into
motion, that by their means he may do his work. Wherefore

---

[29] Thus a trip to the zoo proves that man's *summum bonum* is not
bodily good. The argument is extrinsic and does not reveal the real
reason, as does the "*I answer that*"; but it is a valid argument. The first
premise means we can be more deeply and truly happy than any animal.
What ape can fall in love (as distinct from lust), or weep with joy at
a symphony? This also shows the difference between happiness and
contentment: the lower the animal, the more merely content it is. Slugs
are more content than cats, cats than humans.

[30] St. Thomas means by "navigation" not just consulting naviga-
tional charts but actually sailing.

[31] Cf. Article 7 for a proof of this point.

all goods of the body are ordained to the goods of the soul, as to their end.[32] Consequently happiness, which is man's last end, cannot consist in goods of the body.

Reply Obj. 1. Just as the body is ordained to the soul, as its end, so are external goods ordained to the body itself. And therefore it is with reason that the good of the body is preferred to external goods, which are signified by *riches*, just as the good of the soul is preferred to all bodily goods.[33]. . .

SIXTH ARTICLE

Whether Man's Happiness Consists in Pleasure?

Objection 1. It would seem that man's happiness consists in pleasure. For since happiness is the last end, it is not desired for something else, but other things for it. But this answers to pleasure more than to anything else: *for it is absurd to ask anyone what is his motive in wishing to be pleased* (*Ethic.* x. 2). Therefore happiness consists principally in pleasure and delight [cf. n. 11]. . . .

Objection 3. Further, since desire is for good, it seems that what all desire is best. But all desire delight;[34] both wise and foolish, and even irrational creatures. Therefore delight is the best of all. Therefore happiness which is the supreme good, consists in pleasure.

---

[32] Contrast Hobbes, or any materialist, for whom the reverse is true: the soul is a mere servant to the body. Hobbes says that reason is "the scout for the senses".

[33] The eight Articles here are arranged in a hierarchical order, a scale of values, which is not merely St. Thomas' personal preference. Such an objective hierarchy is a practical necessity to all intelligent moral choices, for most choices are not between a good and an evil but between two competing goods.

[34] Cf. II–II, 35, 4, Reply 2: "No one can live without delight, and that is why a man deprived of spiritual joy goes over to carnal pleasures" (Gilby translation).

On the contrary, Boëthius says (*De Consol.* iii): *Any one that chooses to look back on his past excesses, will perceive that pleasures* [typically] *have a sad ending: and if they can render a man happy, there is no reason why we should not say that the very beasts are happy too.*[35]

→ *I answer that,* Because bodily delights are more generally known, *the name of pleasure has been appropriated to them* (*Ethic.* vii. 13), although other delights excel them:[36] and yet happiness does not consist in them. Because in every thing, that which pertains to its essence is distinct from its proper accident: thus in man it is one thing that he is [by essence] a mortal rational animal, and another that he [by proper (universal and necessary) accident] is a risible [able to laugh] animal. We must therefore consider that every delight is a proper accident resulting from happiness, or from some part of happiness; since the reason that a man is delighted is that he has some fitting good, either in reality, or in hope, or at least in memory. Now a fitting good, if indeed it be the perfect good, is precisely man's happiness: and if it is imperfect, it is a share of happiness, either proximate, or remote, or at least apparent. Therefore it is evident that neither is delight, which results from the perfect good, the very essence of happiness, but something resulting therefrom as its proper accident.[37]. . .

---

[35] Another indication of how far the ancients were from the moderns on happiness: if *eudaimonia*, or *makarios* (in Greek), or *felicitas*, or *beatitudo* (in Latin) meant mere feelings of contentment, this argument would be unintelligible.

[36] As Plato pointed out (*Republic*, Bk. 9), all who have experienced both the greatest bodily delights and the greatest spiritual delights testify to the same results of this dual experiment: that the soul can experience far greater pleasure than the body. (It can experience far greater suffering, too.) All who doubt this simply prove they lack the experience and are in no position to judge.

[37] The essence is the cause of the accident, and the cause cannot be identical with the effect. *Because* a triangle is a three-sided enclosed

Reply Obj. 1. . . . Delight . . . is nothing else than the appetite's rest in good: thus . . . just as good is desired for itself, so delight is desired for itself and not for anything else, if the preposition *for* denote the final cause. But if it denote the formal . . . cause, thus delight is desirable for something else, *i.e.*, for the good, which is the object of that delight, and . . . gives it its form: for the reason that delight is desired is that it is rest in the thing desired. . . .

Reply Obj. 3. All desire delight in the same way as they desire good: and yet they desire delight by reason of the good and not conversely, as stated above (Reply 1). Consequently it does not follow that delight is the supreme and essential good, but that every delight results from some good, and that some delight results from that which is the essential and supreme good.

SEVENTH ARTICLE

Whether Some Good of the Soul Constitutes Man's Happiness?

Objection 3. Further, perfection is something belonging to that which is perfected. But happiness is a perfection of man. Therefore happiness is something belonging to man. But it is not something belonging to the body, as shown above (A. 5). Therefore it is something belonging to the soul; and thus it consists in goods of the soul.

---

plane figure, it must have 180 degrees in its interior angles. *Because* man is a rational animal, he can laugh, pray, sing, etc. And *because* a man really possesses his fitting good, his end, he is pleased and rejoices. Pleasure is *caused* by the good, or part of the good, or a remembered or anticipated good, or an apparent good; therefore pleasure is not the good itself. We have found a proper effect of the *summum bonum*—it will always cause joy—but we have not yet found the *summum bonum* itself.

On the contrary, As Augustine says (*De Doctr. Christ.* i. 22), *that which constitutes the life of happiness is to be loved for its own sake.* But man is not to be loved for his own sake, but whatever is in man is to be loved for God's sake.[38] Therefore happiness consists in no good of the soul.

I answer that, As stated above (Q. 1, A. 8), the end is twofold: namely, the thing itself, which we desire to attain, and the use, namely, the attainment or possession of that thing. If, then, we speak of man's last end, as to the thing itself which we desire as last end, it is impossible for man's last end to be the soul itself or something belonging to it. Because the soul, considered in itself, is as something existing in potentiality: for it becomes knowing actually, from being potentially knowing; and actually virtuous, from being potentially virtuous. Now since potentiality is for the sake of act as for its fulfilment, that which in itself is in potentiality cannot be the last end. Therefore the soul itself cannot be its own last end.[39] . . .

But if we speak of man's last end, as to the attainment or possession thereof, or as to any use whatever of the thing itself desired as an end, thus does something of man, in respect of his soul, belong to his last end: since man attains happiness through his soul. Therefore the thing itself which is desired as end, is that which constitutes happiness, and makes man happy; but the attainment of this thing is called happiness. Consequently we must say that happiness is something be-

---

[38] St. Thomas does not mean man is a means to be used rather than an end to be loved, but that the ultimate reason man is to be loved is not himself but God. For God is (1) man's exemplary formal cause: man is made in God's image. One loves the image because of the original, not vice versa. And (2) God is man's first efficient cause, his Creator. (3) God is also man's final cause, *summum bonum,* or ultimate end, not vice versa.

[39] If the soul were its own end, this would be as if a moving arrow were its own target.

longing to the soul; but that which constitutes happiness is something outside the soul. . . .

Reply Obj. 3. Happiness itself, since it is a perfection of the soul, is an inherent good of the soul; but that which constitutes happiness, viz., which makes man happy, is something outside his soul, as stated above.

EIGHTH ARTICLE

Whether Any Created Good Constitutes Man's Happiness?

Objection 3. Further, man is made happy by that which lulls [satisfies] his natural desire. But man's natural desire does not reach out to a good surpassing his capacity.[40] Since then man's capacity does not include that good which surpasses the limits of all creation, it seems that man can be made happy by some created good.[41] Consequently some created good constitutes man's happiness.

On the contrary, Augustine says (*De Civ. Dei* xix, 26): *As the soul is the life of the body, so God is man's life of happiness: of Whom it is written: "Happy is that people whose God is the Lord"* (Ps 143:15).

I answer that, It is impossible for any created good to constitute man's happiness. For happiness is the perfect good, which lulls [satisfies] the appetite altogether; else it would not be the last end, if something yet remained to be desired. Now the object of the will, *i.e.,* of man's appetite, is the

---

[40] St. Thomas, following St. Augustine, disagrees with this premise (cf. *Confessions* 1, 1: "Thou hast made us for Thyself, and our hearts are restless till they rest in Thee"). Whether it is to be called a natural desire or a supernatural desire, there is in us an inherent desire for God.

[41] Another maxim: "Know then thyself; presume not God to scan. The proper study of mankind is man" (Alexander Pope, *An Essay on Man*). C. S. Lewis replies, "The proper study of mankind is everything."

universal good; just as the object of the intellect is the universal true. Hence it is evident that naught can lull man's will, save the universal good.[42] This is to be found, not in any creature, but in God alone; because every creature has goodness by participation. Wherefore God alone can satisfy the will of man, according to the words of Psalm 102:5: *Who satisfieth thy desire with good things*. Therefore God alone constitutes man's happiness. . . .

Reply Obj. 3. Created good is not less than that good of which man is capable, as of something intrinsic and inherent to him: but it is less than the good of which he is capable, as of an object, and which is infinite. And the participated good which is in an angel, and in the whole universe, is a finite and restricted good.

---

[42] N.b.: St. Thomas does not say universal *goodness*, but the universal *good*. God might be called a "concrete universal" rather than either an abstract universal or a concrete particular.

QUESTION 5

Of Goodness in General[43]

SIXTH ARTICLE

Whether Goodness Is Rightly Divided into
the Virtuous, the Useful, and the Pleasant?[44]

I answer that, . . . in the movement of the appetite, the thing desired that terminates the movement of the appetite relatively, as a means by which something tends towards another, is called the useful; but that sought after as the last thing absolutely terminating the movement of the appetite, as a thing towards which for its own sake the appetite tends, is called the virtuous; for the virtuous is that which is desired for its own sake; but that which terminates the movement of the appetite in the form of rest in the thing desired, is called the pleasant. . . .

---

[43] This question is preliminary to the question of the goodness of God (Question 6). Goodness is one of the five "transcendentals", or universal properties of all being: all that is, is something, is one, is good, is true, and is beautiful.

[44] "The virtuous" (*bonum honestum*) means the right, the intrinsically valuable, the fitting and proper. The thesis that there are only these three kinds of good is radical and practical, for it means that there are only three reasons why anyone should ever do anything: because it is morally virtuous, practically necessary, or fun. How much of what we do is not good by this standard? (E.g., doing things just because "everyone is doing it", or because it is "expected".) St. Thomas' classification of goods is a philosophical justification for a wonderful simplification of our lives.

The Distinction of
Things in Particular

SIXTH ARTICLE

Whether Pain Has the Nature of Evil
More Than Fault Has?

On the contrary, A wise workman chooses a less evil in order to prevent a greater,[45] as the surgeon cuts off a limb to save the whole body. But divine wisdom inflicts pain to prevent fault. Therefore fault is a greater evil than pain.

I answer that, Fault has the nature of evil more than pain has; not only more than pain of sense, consisting in the privation of corporeal goods, which kind of pain appeals to most men; but also more than any kind of pain, thus taking pain in its most general meaning, so as to include privation of grace or glory.[46]

---

[45] St. Thomas is not saying here that it is wise or good to commit a lesser fault to prevent a greater one (for this is never necessary; our own faults are prevented by our own choices, and others' faults are others' faults, not ours), but that it is wise and good sometimes to inflict the lesser *kind* of evil, pain, to prevent the greater kind, fault. Thus punishment, which must be painful in some way, can be morally good if it is both deserved and is aimed at deterring the one punished from future faults. The principle of "the lesser of two evils" means (1) that we often must *tolerate* or allow the lesser evil to prevent the greater one, and (2) that we should sometimes inflict the lesser *kind* of evil to prevent the greater kind (above), but not (3) that we should commit little sins to prevent big sins.

[46] Therefore sin (the evil of fault) is an even greater evil than its punishment (the privation of God's life in the soul, which is present imperfectly in this life by grace and perfectly in the next by glory).

There is a twofold reason for this. The first is that one becomes evil by the evil of fault, but not by the evil of pain, as Dionysius says (*Div. Nom.* iv): *To be punished is not an evil; but it is an evil to be made worthy of punishment.* And this because, since good absolutely considered consists in act, and not in potentiality, and the ultimate act is operation, or the use of something possessed, it follows that the absolute good of man consists in good operation, or the good use of something possessed. Now we use all things by the act of the will. Hence from a good will, which makes a man use well what he has, man is called good, and from a bad will he is called bad. For a man who has a bad will can use ill even the good he has, as when a grammarian of his own will speaks incorrectly. Therefore, because the fault itself consists in the disordered act of the will, and the pain consists in the privation of something used by the will, fault has more of evil in it than pain has.[47]

The second reason can be taken from the fact that God is the author of the evil of pain, but not of the evil of fault. And this is because the evil of pain takes away the creature's good, which may be either something created, as sight, destroyed by blindness, or something uncreated, as by being deprived of the vision of God, the creature forfeits its uncreated good. But the evil of fault is properly opposed to uncreated good: for it is opposed to the fulfillment of the divine will, and to divine love, whereby the divine good is loved for itself, and not only as shared by the creature. Therefore it is plain that fault has more evil in it than pain has.[48]

In other words, the worst evil is not Hell but sin. The conclusion is startling to our sensibilities but demonstrated to our reason.

[47] St. Thomas here includes the fundamental moral insight of Socrates, that it is better to suffer evil than to do it, and that of Kant, that the heart of good (Kant says the *only* intrinsic good) is a good will.

[48] Actively to oppose uncreated good (God Himself) is more evil than to be deprived of it passively.

Of the Cardinal Virtues

SECOND ARTICLE

Whether There Are Four Cardinal Virtues?

On the contrary, Gregory says (*Moral.* ii): *The entire structure of good works is built on four virtues.*

I answer that, Things may be numbered either in respect of their formal principles, or according to the subjects in which they are: and either way we find that there are four cardinal virtues.[49]

For the formal principle of the virtue of which we speak now is good as defined by reason; which good can be considered in two ways. First, as existing in the very act of reason: and thus we have one principal virtue, called *Prudence* [practical wisdom].—Secondly, according as the reason puts its order into something else; either into operations, and then we have *Justice*; or into passions, and then we need two virtues. For the need of putting the order of reason into the passions is due to their thwarting reason: and this occurs in two ways. First, by the passions inciting to something against reason; and then the passions need a curb, which we call *Temperance* [moderation, self-control].

---

[49] St. Thomas is very good at this sort of thing: providing a theoretical outline as a background to explain and justify some traditional list. In primitive societies we nearly always find simple numerical lists (The Ten Terrible Things, The Five Treasures, The Twelve Steps of Mystic Initiation, etc.). The Greeks and medievals raised the concept of order to a higher level of abstraction than mere lists. Modernity tends to see all such traditional order as imposed by the mind, largely because of Kant's "Copernican revolution", and as historically relative, largely because of Hegel's historicism.

Secondly, by the passions withdrawing us from following the dictate of reason, *e.g.*, through fear of danger or toil: and then man needs to be strengthened for that which reason[50] dictates, lest he turn back; and to this end there is *Fortitude* [courage].

In like manner, we find the same number if we consider the subjects[51] of virtue. For there are four subjects of the virtue we speak of now: viz., the power which is rational in its essence, and this is perfected by *Prudence*; and that which is rational by participation,[52] and is threefold, the will, subject of *Justice*, the concupiscible [desiring] faculty, subject of *Temperance*, and the irascible [averting] faculty, subject of *Fortitude*. . . .

---

[50] Note how St. Thomas' classification of all four virtues is determined by their relation to reason. This is surprising only if we forget that St. Thomas meant by "reason" not just reasoning but also insight into reality, understanding truth.

[51] A *subject* of virtue is that in which virtue inheres, that which *has* the virtue.

[52] I.e., sharing reason by obeying reason, as a flying arrow shares the plan and purpose and intelligence of the archer.

Of the Theological Virtues

THIRD ARTICLE

Whether Faith, Hope, and Charity Are Fittingly Reckoned as Theological Virtues?

Objection 2. Further, the theological virtues are more perfect than the intellectual and moral virtues. Now faith is not reckoned among the intellectual virtues, but is something less than a virtue, since it is imperfect knowledge. Likewise hope is not reckoned among the moral virtues, but is something less than a virtue, since it is a passion. Much less therefore should they be reckoned as theological virtues. . . .

On the contrary, The Apostle says (1 Cor 13:13): *Now there remain faith, hope, charity, these three.*

I answer that, As stated above (A. 1), the theological virtues direct man to supernatural happiness in the same way as by the natural inclination man is directed to his connatural end. Now the latter . . . fall[s] short of the order of supernatural happiness, according to 1 Corinthians 2:9: *The eye hath not seen, nor ear heard, neither hath it entered into the heart of man, what things God hath prepared for them that love Him.* Consequently . . . man needed to receive in addition something supernatural to direct him to a supernatural end. First, as regards the intellect, man receives certain supernatural principles, which are held by means of a Divine light: these are the articles of faith, about which is faith.—Secondly, the will is directed to this end, both as to the movement of intention, which tends to that end as something attainable,—and this pertains to hope,—and as to a certain spiritual union, whereby the will is, so to speak, transformed into that end,—and this belongs to charity. . . .

Reply Obj. 2. Faith and hope imply a certain imperfection: since faith is of things unseen, and hope, of things not possessed. Hence faith and hope in things that are subject to human power, fall short of the notion of virtue. But faith and hope in things which are above the capacity of human nature surpass all virtue that is in proportion to man, according to 1 Corinthians 1:25: *The weakness of God is stronger than men.* . . .

Of the Various Kinds of Law

FIRST ARTICLE

Whether There Is an Eternal Law?

I answer that, As stated above (Q. 90, A. 1 *ad* 2; AA.
3, 4), a law is nothing else but a dictate of practical reason
emanating from the ruler who governs a perfect [complete]
community. Now it is evident, granted that the world is
ruled by Divine Providence, as was stated in the First Part
(Q. 22, AA. 1, 2), that the whole community of the universe is governed by Divine Reason. Wherefore the very
Idea of the government of things in God the Ruler of the
universe, has the nature of a law. And since the Divine Reason's conception of things is not subject to time but is eternal, according to Proverbs 8:23, therefore it is that this kind
of law must be called eternal. . . .

SECOND ARTICLE

Whether There Is in Us a Natural Law?

On the contrary, A gloss on Romans 2:14: *When the Gentiles, who have not the* [Mosaic] *law, do by nature those things
that are of the law,* comments as follows: *Although they have
no written law, yet they have the natural law, whereby each one
knows, and is conscious of, what is good and what is evil.*

I answer that, As stated above (Q. 90, A. 1 *ad* 1), law,
being a rule and measure, can be in a person in two ways:
in one way, as in him that rules and measures; in another
way, as in that which is ruled and measured, since a thing
is ruled and measured, in so far as it partakes of the rule

or measure. Wherefore, since all things subject to Divine providence are ruled and measured by the eternal law, as was stated above (A. 1); it is evident that all things partake somewhat of the eternal law, in so far as, namely, from its being imprinted on them, they derive their respective inclinations to their proper acts and ends. Now among all others, the rational creature is subject to Divine providence in the most excellent way, in so far as it partakes of a share of providence, by being provident both for itself and for others. Wherefore it has a share of the Eternal Reason, whereby it has a natural inclination to its proper act and end: and this participation of the eternal law in the [very nature of the] rational creature is called the natural law. Hence the Psalmist after saying (Ps 4:6): *Offer up the sacrifice of justice*, as though someone asked what the works of justice are, adds: *Many say, Who showeth us good things?* in answer to which question he says: *The light of Thy countenance, O Lord, is signed upon us:* thus implying that the light of natural reason, whereby we discern what is good and what is evil, which is the function of the natural law, is nothing else than an imprint on us of the Divine light. It is therefore evident that the natural law is nothing else than the rational creature's participation of the eternal law.[53] . . .

THIRD ARTICLE

Whether there Is a Human Law?

I answer that, As stated above (Q. 90, A. 1, *ad* 2), a law is a dictate of the practical reason. Now it is to be observed that the same procedure takes place in the practical and in the speculative reason: for each proceeds from principles to conclusions, as stated above (*ibid.*). Accordingly we conclude

---

[53] Thus the voice of conscience (natural reason judging good and evil) is the echo of the voice of God, and is therefore sacred and inviolable.

that just as, in the speculative reason, from naturally known indemonstrable principles,[54] we draw the conclusions of the various sciences, the knowledge of which is not imparted to us by nature, but acquired by the efforts of reason, so too it is from the precepts of the natural law, as from general and indemonstrable principles, that the human reason needs to proceed to the more particular determination of certain matters. These particular determinations, devised by human reason, are called human laws.[55]. . .

FOURTH ARTICLE

Whether There Was Any Need for a Divine Law?[56]

I answer that, Besides the natural and the human law it was necessary for the directing of human conduct to have a Divine law. And this for four reasons. First, because . . . man is ordained to an end of eternal happiness. . . .

Secondly . . . on account of the uncertainty of human judgment. . . .

---

[54] Self-evident theoretical axioms like the law of non-contradiction. There are also self-evident practical axioms, both general ("Do good, avoid evil") and specific ("Be just"). These are "the precepts of the natural law", which, since it is in our nature, is also naturally *known*, just as first theoretical principles are.

[55] "Human law" is "positive law", law posited (made) by man. Moral positivism reduces all moral law to this, denying the eternal law and the natural law. A philosopher could admit the natural law without admitting the eternal law, since one could know the effect without knowing the cause; therefore the argument between legal positivism and natural law does not depend only on whether or not God is admitted. St. Thomas would disagree with Dostoyevski's saying, "If God does not exist, everything is permissible."

[56] The divine law is that part of the eternal law which God made known by special revelation.

Thirdly, because . . . man is not competent to judge of interior movements, that are hidden. . . .

Fourthly, because . . . human law cannot punish or forbid all evil deeds. . . .

Of the Natural Law

FIFTH ARTICLE

Whether the Natural Law Can Be Changed?

I answer that, A change in the natural law may be understood in two ways. First, by way of addition. In this sense nothing hinders the natural law from being changed: since many things for the benefit of human life have been added over and above the natural law, both by the Divine law and by human laws.[57]

Secondly, a change in the natural law may be understood by way of subtraction, so that what previously was according to the natural law, ceases to be so. In this sense, the natural law is altogether unchangeable in its first principles: but in its secondary principles, which, as we have said (A. 4), are certain detailed proximate conclusions drawn from the first principles, the natural law . . . may be changed in some particular cases of rare occurrence, through some special causes hindering the observance of such precepts, as stated above (A. 4). . . .

SIXTH ARTICLE

Whether the Law of Nature Can Be Abolished from the Heart of Man?

On the contrary, Augustine says (*Conf.* ii): *Thy law is written in the hearts of men, which iniquity itself effaces not.* But

---

[57] E.g., the Beatitudes and the "evangelical counsels" in the New Testament add significantly to the old law; or there is the obligation to vote in a modern democracy, but not in an ancient monarchy.

the law which is written in men's hearts is the natural law. Therefore the natural law cannot be blotted out.

I answer that, As stated above (AA. 4, 5), there belong to the natural law, first, certain most general precepts, that are known to all; and secondly, certain secondary and more detailed precepts, which are, as it were, conclusions following closely from first principles. As to those general principles, the natural law, in the abstract, can nowise be blotted out from men's hearts. But it[58] is blotted out in the case of a particular action, in so far as reason is hindered from applying the general principle to a particular point of practice, on account of concupiscence or some other passion, as stated above (Q. 77, A. 2).—But as to the other, *i.e.*, the secondary precepts, the natural law can be blotted out from the human heart . . . by vicious customs and corrupt habits, as among some men, theft, and even unnatural vices, as the Apostle states (Rom 1), were not esteemed sinful.[59] . . .

---

[58] I.e., the *knowledge* of the moral law, not the "rectitude" or objective rightness of it.

[59] The greatest harm done by vice is thus its blinding of the reason against even *knowing* good and evil (cf. Jn 7:17). Cf. the blithely self-confident justification of "unnatural vice" today.